AN OWNER'S GUIDE
TO OPERATING A
REALLY SMALL BUSINESS

CREDITS

Editor: Beverly Manber

Layout/Design: ExecuStaff

Cover Design: Kathleen Gadway

Library of Congress 92-54355
ISBN-1-56052-169-4

Limits of Liability and Disclaimer of Warranty

The author and publisher have used their best efforts in preparing this book and make no warranty of any kind, expressed or implied, with regard to the instructions and suggestions contained herein. This book is not intended to render legal or accounting advice. Such advice should be obtained from competent, licensed professionals.

INTRODUCTION TO THE SERIES

This series of books is intended to inform and assist those of you who are in the beginning stages of starting a new small business venture or who are considering such an undertaking.

It is because you are confident of your abilities that you are taking this step. These books will provide additional information and support along the way.

Not every new business will succeed. The more information you have about budgeting, cash flow management, accounts receivables, marketing and employee management, the better prepared you will be for the inevitable pitfalls.

A unique feature of the Crisp Small Business & Entrepreneurship Series is the personal involvement exercises, which give you many opportunities to immediately apply the concepts presented to your own business.

In each book in the series, these exercises take the form of "Your Turn," a checklist to confirm your understanding of the concept just presented and "Ask Yourself . . . ," a series of chapter-ending questions, designed to evaluate your overall understanding or commitment.

In addition, numerous case studies are included, and each book is cross-referenced to others in the series and to other publications.

BOOKS IN THE SERIES

- **Operating a Really Small Business**
  Betty M. Bivins

- **Budgeting: A Primer for Entrepreneurs**
  Terry Dickey

- **Getting a Business Loan: Your Step-By-Step Guide**
  Orlando J. Antonini

- **Nobody Gets Rich Working for Somebody Else: An Entrepreneur's Guide**
  Roger Fritz

- **Marketing Strategies for Small Businesses**
  Richard F. Gerson, Ph.D.

- **Financial Basics for Small Business Success**
  James O. Gill

- **Extending Credit and Collecting Cash: A Small Business Guide**
  Lynn Harrison

- **Avoiding Mistakes in Your New Business**
  David Karlson, Ph.D.

- **Buying Your First Franchise: The Least You Need to Know**
  Rebecca Luhn, Ph.D.

- **Buying a Business: Tips for the First-Time Buyer**
  Ronald J. McGregor

- **Your New Business: A Personal Plan for Success**
  Charles L. Martin, Ph.D.

- **Managing the Family Business: A Guide for Success**
  Marshall W. Northington, Ph.D.

ACKNOWLEDGMENTS

The author wishes to acknowledge and thank the following people for their invaluable input, review and behind-the-scenes assistance: Patricia E. Pfeiffer, APD, and Edward Z. Hane, Ph.D., Principals of Personnel Consulting Group; Anita Rowe, Ph.D., Partner, Gardenswartz & Rowe Management Consultants; Hal Lampert, CPA, Lampert & Eskridge Accounting Services; and Chris Weiss, Owner, PDQ Secretarial Services.

CONTENTS

CONTENTS (continued)

PREFACE

When I started my one-person technical writing company ten years ago, I looked around for help in running it. I found lots of advice. An endless stream of magazines, books, videotapes, and cassettes told me everything from how to use my time—delegate to my staff—to how to spend my advertising budget wisely—research the market and then select the most appropriate media mix.

Although the material was intended for what the authors called "small" businesses, most of it proved useless since I was my own staff and I had no advertising budget. It didn't take me long to discover that what these publications meant by small businesses were companies that grossed at least $500,000 a year—and often two or three times that amount. As owner of a company that produced a gross annual income of about $30,000 its first year, I continued sporadically to hunt for advice on how to organize my time and apportion my limited financial resources so that I, and my business, could survive.

While I never found the advice I needed, I survived and my company has slowly, but steadily, increased its annual gross income to where it now pays me, two to four writers, and a network of subcontractors to whom I delegate part of the workload.

Along the way, while I was learning how to run my really small business profitably, I also discovered the many satisfactions of the entrepreneurial life. It's great to be your own boss!

Although I was fortunate to avoid making any crucial—read disastrous—errors, I would have made fewer mistakes, worked fewer "8-day" weeks, and probably expanded more quickly, if I'd had the benefit of advice that applied to a company the size of mine. The information in this book, compiled from the experiences of a considerable number of owners of businesses with one to ten employees, will help prevent you from wasting your all too limited commodities—time, energy and money. At the very least, you won't have to reinvent the wheel.

Before you dive into this, you need to know something of what this book does and, equally important, what it doesn't do.

1. IT DOESN'T tell you how to start a new business. While start-up and operating procedures overlap to some extent (recordkeeping, for instance), there are many differences between the two. In some ways, businesses are like automobiles—it's one thing to get them started and quite another to keep them running smoothly.

   IT DOES assume you're past the initial start-up stage, and are ready to modify your procedures, product or service, and even your goals if necessary, to make your company more efficient, productive and profitable.

   It also assumes that you have met all federal, state and local requirements for such basic matters as safety, insurance, worker's compensation, taxes and any applicable environmental considerations. If you have doubts or questions about any of these or similar regulations, consult the appropriate regulatory agency in your locality, your accountant or CPA and, where necessary, an attorney or other expert. Since requirements vary greatly from business to business and area to area, this book couldn't begin to offer the kinds of specific information and guidelines applicable to every business.

2. IT DOESN'T give you a recipe for guaranteed success. Success requires a quality product or service, a need or desire for that product or service among potential buyers, an available market and willingness on your part to work hard.

   IT DOES offer a great deal of practical information that will enable you to create your own recipe, assuming you have these necessary ingredients.

3. IT DOESN'T provide a list of steps, set of procedures or cut and dry answers to predetermined questions.

   IT DOES provide guidelines, options, examples and suggestions designed to help you develop and exercise the judgment necessary for making informed decisions for your company.

Specifically, it contains information on concrete topics. Included where appropriate are practical examples for three broad business categories: MANUFACTURING, SELLING (wholesale or retail) and SERVICES that support either or both of the first two categories. Since these major classifications include all possible types and sizes of business, you will discover many examples to apply or adapt to your own firm.

Overview

Each chapter in this book discusses one aspect essential for operating your business efficiently.

Chapter One: Managing Your Product or Service deals with maintaining control over the product or service you sell: quality, costs, inventory, corrective action and your competition.

Chapter Two: Managing Your Business Operations covers the basics involved in customer service, planning ahead, finances, suppliers and/or employees, time management and routine maintenance of equipment and facilities.

Chapter Three: Surviving Common Pitfalls, Pratfalls and Major Disasters provides solid information about avoiding or recovering from problems you can't foresee, errors of judgment and events over which you have no control.

Chapter Four: Developing Marketing and Advertising Systems offers practical ways to identify your potential customers, develop a workable marketing and advertising plan, and track the results of these efforts.

Chaper Five: Expanding Your Business explains how to increase cash flow and profits, product line or service and space or equipment, as needed.

By completing the *Your Turn* and *Ask Yourself* exercises, as well as the worksheets that are in many of the chapters, you can relate the chapter ideas to your business and apply or adapt specific points and guidelines to your company. Used consistently, these practices and worksheets can help you attain success more easily and quickly than you might otherwise do.

While it doesn't solve all problems you encounter, this book helps you survive some of the difficulties that lie in wait around every corner. It also allows you to gain the experience and knowledge necessary to operate your small business successfully and to enjoy the process.

CHAPTER
ONE

MANAGING YOUR PRODUCT OR SERVICE

CHAPTER ONE

MAINTAIN MOMEN-TUM

Guiding Principle: Maintain your initial momentum!

It's great when a new business starts well and achieves a measure of success quickly. But sitting on that initial success can be fatal to your company's health. How? It's extremely tempting to sit back, and wait comfortably for the world to arrive on your doorstep.

In a word, don't. If we lived in an unchanging world, or even the slower paced one of a hundred years ago, relaxing your vigilance after a strong start might work. But we live in a world of rapid and constant change. This means that the chances are great that your clients, your market, your competition and probably the technology behind your product line or service are not the same as they were even a few months or a year ago.

In practical terms, this translates to keeping a continuous and wary eye on whatever you produce and sell. The needs of your clients or customers may have shifted significantly according to changes in the economic climate, your marketing area may be undergoing a transition from residential to industrial or from one type of population to another and your competition may have changed or added to its previous offerings in a way that impacts your company. Above all, the increasingly rapid pace of technological changes, including those seemingly far removed from your business, can create ripples or a domino effect that causes dramatic changes in a remarkably short time.

This chapter focuses on the elements essential for maintaining momentum in managing your product or service:

▶ Maintain and Improve Quality

▶ Control Costs

▶ Improve Product or Service

▶ Develop Corrective Action Strategies

▶ Keep Informed about New Products or Services

MAINTAIN AND IMPROVE QUALITY

The key term here, for a business of any size, is *quality.* Owners who keep a constant and vigilant eye on the quality of whatever they produce are certain to end up in the winner's circle. Whether their field is manufacturing, selling or providing a service, those who assume that quality, once established, can be taken largely for granted will—sooner or later—find themselves in difficulties.

Although quality control may sound forbidding—costly, complex and time consuming—it can be surprisingly easy and inexpensive. This is especially true when rework time, spoiled materials and lost customers are figured into the cost of doing business. Where large firms may require a full scale Quality Assurance Department, careful monitoring of those who provide raw materials, supplies and services, plus equally careful selection and maintenance of plant and/or office equipment is usually sufficient to assure a small business of consistent control over quality.

Monitor Your Suppliers

While many small companies use outside suppliers for a variety of products and services, a practical monitoring list will itemize only four or five materials and/or suppliers crucial to controlling quality. Specifically, the monitoring process begins with identifying the basic products, raw materials and services most important to producing what you sell.

In manufacturing, the list will probably consist of basic raw materials and components. In a retail operation, it will contain the merchandise your customers need most, as well as your best selling items—the two are not necessarily the same. In a service business, you may have listed essential supplies and outside services. With a brief, specific list in hand you can perform regular monitoring of invoices, packing slips, material tags, etc., in considerably less time than you expect.

It's easy to assume that a regular supplier will continue to send what you originally ordered. But a small manufacturing company that sold its products to distributors discovered that raw material carrying the same name on the invoice had material tags that told a different story. When the alert business owner inquired about the difference, the supplier said it was an improvement over the former material; the manufacturer's tests however, showed the new material to be considerably less durable than the original. Monitoring protected both product quality and the company's reputation.

In another instance, a previously outstanding word processing service produced some 25 pages of inferior work—full of errors and incorrect in format. The business owner's habit of monitoring all outside vendors resulted in quick discovery and correction. In this instance the supplier had hired another person to do some of the work, but hadn't monitored the work produced after the first project had proved satisfactory.

Choose the Best Suppliers

One of the best ways to choose suppliers who meet your requirements for quality, cost effectiveness and reliable, on-time delivery is to use the results of your monitoring process to weed out those who can't or don't produce what you want when you need it. This selection process may be all that is necessary for some businesses.

Other methods to keep abreast of sources for materials and services can be equally useful where applicable to your specific business:

- ► *Trade shows* identify, display and demonstrate new materials, services, components and equipment as they appear in the market.

- ► *Trade journals* provide similar information and may also provide written comparisons or evaluations which, for small business owners, can take the place of expensive in-house research and testing programs.

- ► *Advertisements that arrive in the mail,* usually directed to your type of business, identify local suppliers as well as large, national firms. Sometimes these flyers, catalogs and brochures arrive in floods; try to resist the urge to toss them out. Instead, toss them into a file folder; when time permits or need dictates, go through the file to locate the supplies or services you need.

► *Telephone inquiries* arrive, frequently at inconvenient times, from individuals seeking employment and firms seeking your business. When callers ask about employment, request a brief resumé and, if appropriate, samples of their work. Sometimes you never hear from them again; those who send what you ask for are likely prospects. As for those who try to actually sell you supplies over the phone—DON'T buy. While legitimate suppliers, especially those whose companies are new, may introduce themselves by phone and offer to send you a catalog of their offerings, those who try to get you to buy anything sight unseen are too often scams of one kind or another.

If you maintain a file of possible suppliers over a period of months or years, you will develop a network of individuals and firms that can supply what you need, when you need it, at a reasonable cost.

Purchase and Maintain the Best Equipment You Can Afford

This may seem obvious. But when cash flow is sluggish, an exceedingly tempting way for a small business to save money is to buy equipment of lesser quality. A similar temptation under such circumstances is not to buy maintenance contracts on new equipment or to let them lapse after a year. While it's not always possible to purchase the top of the line equipment, failure to buy the best possible and keep service contracts in force will quickly short-circuit your ability to produce top quality products and services.

Most business owners who depend on machinery to produce what they sell are acutely aware of the need for a regular maintenance schedule. Even when they have maintenance contracts, an amazing number of people, including some who take superb care of plant equipment, do not apply the same principle to their office equipment.

Copy machines are an excellent example. Cleaned and checked regularly by the service technician (at no cost under a service contract), most copy machines will turn out clean, clear copies of your business forms, letters and other paper-work for many years with very little downtime; lack of proper maintenance, however, will result in frequent breakdowns, constant frustrations and shorter machine life.

Your Turn

Answer the following:

► List the materials, supplies, and outside services essential for maintaining quality in your business.

► Do you currently have a plan for monitoring your suppliers?

► Have you established a plan to purchase and maintain the best possible equipment? What equipment is on that list?

Worksheet: Monitoring Suppliers

Suppliers Name: _____

Material, Product or Service: _____

Monitoring Method	Dates Checked					
Completed On Time						
Invoice						
Material Label/Tag						
Packing Slip						
Product or Work Produced						
Production Test						
Other						
Other						

Ratings: 1 = Outstanding   2 = Good   3 = Satisfactory   4 = Reject

Notes:

CONTROL COSTS

Cost control measures, important for success in any business, are vital for companies whose volume and profit margins are likely to be relatively small. Fortunately, there are some practical ways to control costs without sacrificing quality, investing in complicated accounting procedures or spending large amounts of time. In particular, it is nearly always possible to reduce costs by improving the quality and efficiency of systems and procedures and by upgrading equipment.

CAUTION: It would be easy to dismiss some of the best control measures as too simplistic or insignificant to make a difference. As any accountant knows, the difference between positive and negative cash flow can often be measured in pennies, rather than dollars, and in small, specific changes, rather than in sweeping, global ones.

Make Plant and Office Systems and Procedures More Efficient

When you first start a business, it's a triumph to establish systems and procedures that work well enough to keep the business running. After the start-up period, it's extremely easy to allow your first method of doing things to become *the* way, especially since the demands on your time and energy are endless. But "first" doesn't always mean "best," and "workable" doesn't necessarily mean "most efficient." Therefore, after those first hectic months or years, take a close look at production methods and what I call "delivery systems" for whatever you sell.

In their second year, a small manufacturing firm (a husband, wife and two employees) found that a factory-installed guardrail on a conveyor belt wasn't quite long enough to prevent certain parts from falling to the floor in larger numbers than other parts did. Insignificant at first, the cost of those extra rejects increased to significant proportions as production increased. A relatively minor adjustment in the location of that guardrail resulted in an instant and welcome decrease in costs.

In another instance, a two-person consulting and training company that designed and conducted workshops for clients struggled for the first two years under an ever increasing load of client files, session folders and stacks of handouts. Finally, when the piles of paper threatened to engulf the office, one partner advanced the idea of using interlocking stacking trays, a different color for each client, to hold the folders and handouts. Lined up on worktables against the back wall of the office, the stacks of brightly colored trays instantly turned chaos into order, looked attractive and, as a fringe benefit, made available a considerable amount of table top space—formerly hidden under disorderly papers. Most important was the fact that both partners spent much less time filing, hunting for materials and organizing workshop sessions—a marked cost reduction for a company whose profit depends, to a large extent, on the amount of time invested by the partners.

In the desktop publishing field, one of the most unpredictable and wildly varying costs is the rate that graphics designers and other illustrators charge for their services. Finding someone with the necessary skills at a reasonable cost is like plowing through quicksand over an uncharted landscape. One way to get comparable quotes is to prepare a portfolio with samples of basic types of illustrations you use most often. Potential illustrators can examine these to make a bid on a project requiring X number of drawings similar in type, size and complexity to some or all of the portfolio examples. While the range may still be fairly wide, bids based on comparable samples will enable you to make choices that help you control costs.

Update and Upgrade Equipment

Much equipment—fax machines, computers, copy machines, cash registers, production machinery, telephone systems, word processors, etc.—becomes more efficient, reliable, cost effective and sometimes less costly in a few years. Naturally, there are exceptions to this; sometimes a small company simply can't afford to replace or upgrade equipment when it likes. Yet, when practical, this can be an important way to control costs, especially if the new equipment can perform more functions or can save time through faster operation.

Replacing an ordinary cash register with a computerized model, for example, can speed up transactions, make record-keeping more accurate, and keep track of inventory all at the same time—a sizable saving in time and money for many small retail firms. Even if you can't afford new purchases right away, it's a good idea to examine your present equipment, check costs of replacement and determine to what extent new models could help you control costs. Such advance analysis can prepare you to act quickly when opportunity knocks.

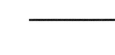

Your Turn

Examine your operation closely and answer the following:

▶ List one production or office procedure that you can modify or replace to require less time and effort for the same results.

▶ List one piece of equipment that you can modify or replace to require less time and effort to achieve the same results.

▶ Which pieces of equipment have you upgraded and updated?

▶ In what order is the rest of your equipment to be upgraded and updated?

Worksheet: Rating Cost Control Strategies

As you use this worksheet to rate the efficiency of your cost control strategies, make estimates of time and money saved when exact figures aren't applicable or easily identified.

EQUIPMENT

Name of equipment adjusted, modified or replaced:

_____

Problem: Defective parts or sheets, slow production, etc.:

_____

Amount/number of defects per hour, day, month, etc., or present production rate:

_____

Reduction in defects after adjustment, modification or replacement:

_____

Amount of money/time saved:

_____

SPACE/MATERIALS

Space or materials reorganized:

_____

Purpose (convenience, faster handling, increase space, etc.):

_____

Amount of time, money and/or handling saved by the reorganization:

_____

IMPROVE PRODUCT OR SERVICE

There's an old saying, "If it ain't broke, don't fix it." While this adage contains the proverbial grain of truth that change, merely for the sake of change, is a waste of time and money, following it can breed an attitude of complacency that sooner or later will reduce profits or prevent your business from growing at the rate you wish. Change, in the form of improved products or services, is essential for you to keep up with the rapid advance of technology, stay ahead of your competition, and, yes, to keep your customers interested in your products or services.

Some changes, especially in product packaging, are no more than cosmetic. Others are dictated by current fashions, rather than a desire for improvement. On a long term basis, while they may increase customer demand temporarily, changes such as these are not likely to improve your bottom-line profits; on the other hand, genuine improvements are likely to yield solid benefits for you and your customers. The owner of even the smallest one-person firm can discover a surprising number of ways to improve products and/or services: locate better materials, drop low profit items and services, add new products or services, or modify current offerings.

Examine New Products and Suppliers to Locate Better Materials

New materials for all kinds of products and services arrive on the market continually—sometimes in bewildering quantities and nearly always accompanied by literature that claims enormous advantages for the new line. Clearly, you need to view such claims with a wary eye. But trying new materials, especially at little or no cost to you, is an excellent and timesaving way to sort out what's *new and good* from what's merely *new.*

A manufacturer of plastic toys used a variety of coloring agents in his products, partly for distinguishing one type of toy from another, but mostly for customer appeal. Although all materials were rated safe for children, some had a limited range of colors; others had a tendency to fade. After trying a number of new coloring agents, the company found one that was ideal; it came in a wide range of colors and testing showed that fading was minimal or nonexistent. This company was lucky enough to find something that improved products and also increased customer appeal.

In another instance, a wholesaler who had been using a particular line of packing boxes was not inclined to try the boxes made by a company just starting up. But the offer of boxes in several sizes on a free trial basis was too good to pass up; this wholesaler quickly discovered that the new boxes, which had reinforced bottoms for the same price as the ones without reinforcement that she had used for three years, resulted in significantly fewer returns of damaged goods. The new supplier had a new customer.

A beauty salon owner, who had tried out a large number of shampoos when she first opened her shop, settled on products supplied by two different companies. Over the next two years, she tried and discarded approximately fifty new shampoos that claimed to do almost everything except actually set the customer's hair. Finally, however, one came on the market that did, in fact, give more body to thin hair and helped prevent split hair ends in dry hair. This small business owner's continuous search for better materials ultimately helped her to provide better service to her customers.

Drop Unprofitable Products or Services

This can be more difficult than you may realize. After all, product *X* or service *Y* was one that helped you launch your business; surely sometime, somewhere, there will be just the right market or customer to turn it into a high profit item. How long do you have to wait to discover that time you spend in producing low profit lines is almost entirely wasted?

The manufacturer of plastic toys and a small mom-and-pop retail grocery operation illustrate this point. The toy manufacturer kept producing a low-profit line of toys simply because they seemed to go with other items he produced. The grocery store owners kept giving shelf space to two or three items that brought in little or no profit because they seemed to belong with other products. The manufacturer finally dropped his low-profit toys when manufacturing costs went up. The grocers got the message after throwing out another batch of outdated goods and realizing that they could use the wasted shelf space to hold more of their high-profit items.

I'm my own best—or worst—example of this point. I was convinced that offering typesetting services, as well as technical writing and illustrations, would pay off someday. Although getting typesetting done right, at the price originally quoted, was a headache from the start, I persisted—out of the conviction that I could hire the services I needed. Five years later, after a particularly frustrating time with costs, quality and production time on a relatively large job, and after I sat down and *really* figured out how much time I'd spent getting the typesetting done right, I realized that I'd been working for around $5.00 per hour—and aging a month every day until the job was finished! Who needs that kind of aggravation? Not I. Typesetting services went out the window the next day.

Add New Products or Services, One at a Time

To do this, you have to monitor your market regularly, as well as keep track of costs—which you're doing anyway, right? But here's an area where really small businesses often have a decided advantage over larger ones, whose production and marketing costs for launching new products and services can reach astronomical heights. Small businesses can frequently launch trail balloons without drying up their cash flow or putting themselves at risk of bankruptcy. You can also get a good deal of advertising or marketing mileage out of a new offering. This provides a natural opportunity to contact former customers, for instance, and can be ideal to target a new group of potential customers. But be careful. Ideas for new products or services sometimes arrive in clusters, rather than one at a time; this can lead to overenthusiasm and, ultimately, to disappointment. One-at-a-time is truly the watchword for this approach to improving your offering.

Since each piece of his furniture was unique, a builder of custom furniture had no "product line." He saw some attractive examples of hand painted borders and similar decorations of furniture at a home show. The builder contacted the artists and arranged for them to perform the same types of painting for his clients at a mutually profitable rate. This business that didn't seem suited for adding new products was able to do so in an unexpected way.

Retailers usually find it relatively easy to add new products. But they must give careful thought to whether a new product or product line is compatible enough with their present line to appeal to their regular customers. If the item is quite different, they must make sure there is a potential market for that type of product.

Adding a new service is easier for some service businesses than others. A professional consultant who specializes in one particular area may not be able to add another kind of service. An automobile repair business, consisting of the owner and three mechanics, did only engine and ignition system work for many years; when a transmission specialist applied for a job, the owner immediately thought of his extra, seldom used repair bay, and decided to add the new service. At the end of the year, he found that his gross profits had increased by 14 percent, largely from the addition of transmission service.

Modify Your Current Offerings

Making changes in your present product line or services can improve quality, enhance your company's image, or increase cosmetic appeal to customers. Large businesses use this approach all the time, changing packaging, ingredients, colors and sizes with sometimes bewildering frequency. Small companies can often do the same on a smaller and less costly scale.

A husband and wife team who made high quality silk flowers for specialty firms recently offered two of their most popular flowers in a new color— burgundy. Despite the fact that only one or two real plants produced anything similar in color, their modification has become immensely popular, especially with hostesses who want centerpieces to match their linens.

A highly successful delicatessen made submarine sandwiches in two sizes—large ones on a big french roll and small ones on half of a french roll; the large ones were immense and the small ones were quite small. As an experiment, the owners offered submarines that weren't submarine shaped at all; they were middle-sized sandwiches on ordinary round buns. These turned out to be very popular with their women customers, who wanted something substantial but not oversized.

At first, two friends who worked together as graphics artists had to use the least expensive materials they could find. When they were able to deliver drawings and page layouts on more expensive durelene and on art boards, the quality of the reproductions improved, as did their image as professionals.

Your Turn

Answer the following:

► Identify possible improvements of your product or service, regardless of whether they are feasible or not.

► List one or two potential improvements most practical for your business.

► List three new products and suppliers that may be helpful to your business.

► List all of your products and services. Put a check by the low profit ones.

Worksheet: Tracking Sales Performance
of New or Improved Product or Service

Make a separate worksheet for each product or service introduced.

Name of Product or Service: _____

Date Introduced: _____

Tracking Period (six months, etc.): _____

New Target Groups	Sales Record for Each Month					
	1	2	3	4	5	6
MARKET NO. 1 Description: Advertising Used:						
MARKET NO. 2 Description: Advertising Used:						
MARKET NO. 3 Description: Advertising Used:						

DEVELOP CORRECTIVE ACTION STRATEGIES

All businesses make mistakes. Even if you keep a close eye on every aspect of your business or do all the work yourself, errors occur. If you plan ahead for the inevitable by developing strategies to correct problems with your product or service, you can gain an advantage over your competition who might be plunging ahead, without concern and without providing for picking up the pieces if something goes wrong. Corrective action plans may be the least of your worries when your business is new; the longer you are in business, the more opportunities you will have to make mistakes. This kind of planning is truly the "stitch in time that saves nine"—to say nothing of pleasing and keeping your customers.

The question, of course, is what type of corrective action planning is right for you. Ideally, there would be a neat list of answers to this question that would apply to all small businesses. The truth is that each business is susceptible to making mistakes, unique to the nature of that business, the personality of the owner or owners, and the specific circumstances surrounding each error—to say nothing of the differences among customers.

Fortunately, there are both preventive and corrective planning strategies available to help lessen the negative impact of whatever goes wrong. One such strategy is to maintain an emergency fund; another is to plan a policy, in advance, to compensate clients for problems you can't correct; a third is to establish a customer contact policy for dealing with delays in delivery of products or services.

Establish an Emergency Fund

I know. You need every dime to run your business. You can't afford to have even the smallest sum sitting idle. The truth is that you can't afford *not* to set aside money, however small the amount may be, to help correct mistakes. The difficulty is often a matter of perception: insurance is a necessity, but an emergency fund is a frill. Well, think about it a moment. What is insurance, but an advance payment of an emergency fund? One relatively painless way to establish your fund is to earmark a small percentage of gross profits, perhaps two percent, to go into a separate bank account. At the rate of $20.00 for every $1,000 of profit, that account would accumulate several hundred dollars in a fairly short time—enough to help correct a number of mistakes.

A manufacturer of rubber stamps usually handled small orders. But the day came when a word was spelled incorrectly on a large order. The company had to do the entire job over at a cost of several hundred dollars.

A neighborhood toy store, in business only a year, operated on a very small profit margin. When two toys, stocked for the holiday season, failed to sell, the company's contingency fund covered most of the loss.

A milling company cut a customer's expensive aluminum stock to the wrong measurements; he had to replace the material and do the work again. The partners scraped up the extra money to correct their mistake, but it wiped out two months of profit. They established an emergency fund as soon as the company recovered from its loss.

Establish a Policy to Compensate Clients for Defective Products or Inadequate Service that Can't Be Corrected

Chief among complaints the public makes about large firms is that they don't care what happens to a customer once the sale is made, or that the service is terrible. There is more than a grain of truth in this. It's harder for large firms than for small ones to handle day-to-day problems with defective merchandise or poor service. Management of large companies, often too far removed from the customer to handle these problems, may have many layers of middle management people between the policy makers and the employees in daily contact with the public.

Because of this—and in spite of the customer service "800" hotlines designed to compensate for the problems inherent in a large-sized company—small firms have a real advantage. In small companies, management is usually right on the firing line; they are well aware of what can and does go wrong, which means that they are in a better position to compensate their customers. The first step is to be aware that more people will take their business elsewhere because they feel they haven't been treated fairly, than because of defective products. The second step is to develop a simple, informal policy for correcting the problems when they occur.

If a manufacturing firm produces a defective product, it's standard practice for them to absorb the cost. It's also fairly common to offer to remake the item on a high priority basis. But the customer may still be dissatisfied unless the company does something extra, which shows concern for the customer.

One company has a policy of automatically offering a hefty 20 percent discount on the customer's next order. Another remakes the defective item and, where appropriate, delivers 10 to 20 percent more of the item than the customer ordered. These companies, who make their fair share of mistakes, retain most of their customers through these policies.

A stationery firm that specializes in selling personalized letterheads, memos, etc., has a policy that they accept any order the customer returns for any reason—including such gems as "I've decided I don't like the type size" or "I know this is what I ordered, but I don't like the way it looks."

I am a frequent customer at a fast-food sandwich franchise. One morning when I went in to order a sandwich, there were no other customers in the shop. However, three people were deep in discussion; one was the manager, another was probably the service man for a drink dispensing machine, and the third was a stranger. After I stood at the counter for nearly five minutes, I finally asked in a peevish voice if "someone could take time out to make me a sandwich." The stranger wheeled around and promptly took care of me. When I paid, the price was only half of what it should have been and I said so. The stranger, who I learned is the owner, gave me a big smile and said, "Today, that's all you owe. We should have taken your order much sooner!" He couldn't repair the mistake, but he certainly compensated for the poor service and, in the process, kept a customer who might otherwise have gone elsewhere.

Establish a Customer Contact System to Handle Unavoidable Delays in Meeting Deadlines

This point, like the preceding one, is concerned with making and keeping your customers satisfied. The best way, of course, is to provide the correct product or service and to deliver it on time. Unfortunately, this just isn't possible one hundred percent of the time. Don't you wish it were? Delivery delays are among the problems that plague every business.

An apology is mandatory, of course, and the sooner the better when you know there will be a delay. But a surprising number of people seem to believe that an honest explanation of the delay is either nobody's business or it will somehow tarnish the company's reputation or image. Rubbish! What really turns customers off is the lack of an explanation. It leaves them feeling that the delay is unnecessary or that you don't value their business. The explanation doesn't have to be long, detailed or damaging to anyone's reputation in your's or the customer's company. It does have to be the *truth,* told simply and in sufficient detail to let the customer know what happened.

If an order will be late because one of your suppliers failed to deliver needed raw materials on time, say so. You don't have to point the finger at the guilty person or firm; you don't have to sound as though you're making up an excuse. In situations like this, one manufacturer always adds this simple statement to his explanation: "You and I both have to suffer the inconvenience this time, but it will be a long time before I trust this particular supplier again, if ever!" He says that most customers realize that the delay really couldn't be helped, and feel that the manufacturer is on their side, not the supplier's.

The above explanation will also serve you if one of your suppliers fails to deliver an item on time. But suppose the problem was really that you forgot to order what your customer wanted—why not say so? It won't make most customers decide that you're an idiot. After all, they've forgotten to do something now and then themselves. It will make most of them feel better about the delay—and you—because you admitted to making a mistake. If anything, you may discover that you have gone up in the customer's estimation, because of your frankness.

Service companies may have more difficulty handling delays because there are likely to be fewer suppliers to blame. When a service company, such as a printer, has made a commitment to deliver a job on a certain date, but other projects or unexpected problems intervene, it's best to tell it like it is. With practice, it gets easier for the owner or manager to say, "My estimate was wrong. It's my fault, but your job won't be ready until ten days later than the date I gave you." The firm may lose an occasional customer because of that delay, but in the long run it will come out ahead. Customers seldom say anything directly but, more often than not, they develop confidence in companies and people who aren't afraid to admit their errors.

Your Turn

Answer the following:

► What is your policy for compensating customers for uncorrectable errors?

► Have you established a specific system for handling delays?

► Have you established an emergency fund?

Worksheet: Establishing Corrective Action Policies and Plans

CORRECTIVE ACTION POLICIES

1. Policy for correcting defects/errors in products/services:

   _____

2. Policy for compensating customers for defects/errors that cannot be corrected:

   _____

3. Policy for compensating customers for late delivery of products/services:

   _____

SPECIFIC TYPES OF DEFECTS/ERRORS

☐ 1. Supplier   ☐ 5. Production   ☐ 9. Other:
☐ 2. Workmanship   ☐ 6. Procedure   _____
☐ 3. Human   ☐ 7. Scheduling   _____
☐ 4. Equipment   ☐ 8. Materials   _____

PROCEDURE TO IMPLEMENT POLICY AND CORRECT DEFECT/ERROR

Identify WHO is to perform corrective action, WHAT is to be done, HOW it is to be done, WHEN it is to be completed, and the PLAN to prevent it from happening again.

WHO: _____

WHAT: _____

HOW: _____

WHEN: _____

PLAN: _____

KEEP INFORMED ABOUT NEW PRODUCTS OR SERVICES

Avoid tunnel vision. Your most diligent efforts to improve your product line or services may be wasted if new and better or more appealing products or services in your field appear on the market while your eyes are glued to your own current offerings. Examples of tunnel vision abound in large companies. For example, consider the computer industry, where a company busily concentrating on improving its own products or software can find itself eclipsed in a matter of months after a new or significantly upgraded product line appears.

It would be comforting to hear that this problem didn't apply to very small companies, but it does. Sometimes it's even worse in small firms, because they seldom have access to the kind of capital required to catch up when the market has leaped ahead to embrace the latest developments.

The commercial art and graphics field offers a case in point. At one time, the vast majority of illustrations and drawings were produced by trained artists or technical illustrators. With the advent of graphics software and computer-aided design (CAD) programs, the need for such trained artists and illustrators has plummeted dramatically. Those who didn't or can't adapt to the new technology are struggling or out of business. Those who did adapt have survived and are doing well, or in some cases, better than ever.

While there is no gimmick or magical system to keep you abreast of new developments in your field, owners rely too often on news items or informal networking; better, more efficient ways are available at reasonable cost: subscriptions to appropriate periodicals, membership in organizations and regular attendance at trade shows or conventions.

Subscribe to Appropriate Periodicals

The key phrase here is "read them consistently." Many new business owners subscribe to various magazines and newsletters that apply to their field—sometimes too many. However, these publications have a tendency to stack up on a desk until they are filed away, out of sheer desperation when the volume becomes overwhelming—"to be read later." Since *later* easily becomes *never,* the subscription money is wasted. Worse, the business owner loses the opportunity to learn about what's new in a particular field.

Practical Use of Periodicals

The first step to make practical use of periodicals is to weed out the least useful ones—those that duplicate information available elsewhere, aren't particularly timely, have only a peripheral application to your business or are simply too long. The principle is simple. If you subscribe to five periodicals and read none of them, you learn nothing; if you subscribe to two and read or scan through them consistently, you can glean a surprising amount of useful information.

The second step, regardless of whether you are in a manufacturing, sales or service field, is to find and hoard those odd moments when you can't possibly work on large projects, and use them faithfully to do your required reading. I like to read during lunch. I'm able to keep up with several catalogs, as well as two short, report type magazines—one for small businesses in general and one with a specific application to my business— by spending an average of fifteen to twenty minutes a day, three or four days a week. I used to also take a business newspaper, but canceled it when I realized that anything arriving every day was more than I could handle.

Two other excellent ways to sandwich reading time into your schedule are at night before you go to bed and, if your work requires extended travel by plane or train, while you are on the way to and from your destination. A partner in a specialized sales firm, who does a lot of customer contact work, carries a briefcase bulging with recent periodicals on her trips; she invariably returns to the office with new ideas and useful information. She feels that while this type of reading during her plane trips isn't too demanding, she uses her time constructively. She also claims that reading in her hotel room in the evening ensures a good night's sleep.

Join Essential Organizations

Even if you are not much of a joiner, membership in a technical, professional, service and/or trade organization can yield a remarkably large amount of information about what's new in your field. Sometimes you will get it from speakers at regularly scheduled meetings, but equally often from person-to-person contacts, over lunch or dinner, before a speaker begins.

While this type of pick-up information isn't always as reliable as what you read in a periodical, it's more timely, and sometimes leads to extended lines of communications between people and firms in related fields. Usually, these organizations hold meetings once a month over breakfast, lunch or dinner, making business use of time that most people would spend out of the office anyway.

The husband and wife owners of a small bakery who had found that most of the information in the trade journal they took applied to much larger concerns than theirs, decided to join a trade organization in their area. Within six months, they had heard of, and tracked down, a new piece of mixing equipment that paid for itself almost overnight by saving them a significant amount of preparation time.

The owners of a small, three-person firm that specializes in training new employees to perform various office and clerical tasks, heard a speaker at their local chapter of a national organization for trainers explain a method for incorporating videotapes into training programs. At first, they thought it was interesting, but not practical for them. However, when they signed a contract to train a large number of a client's new employees whose command of English was limited, they remembered the session on videotapes. For a relatively low cost, they modified the videotape approach in the training program for this client. This proved to be so successful that they received a number of inquiries from other firms and, ultimately, a substantial amount of new business.

Attend Conventions and Trade Shows Regularly

Product and equipment manufacturers, in particular, organize conventions and trade shows to display their new wares and attract new customers. These can be gold mines of information about new offerings in the marketplace. Attending two or three of these a year, even if travel time is required, can provide an enormous amount of information about a wide range of products in a very short time—usually at a moderate cost. There's always a question of how to afford the time, but perhaps a more productive way to look at it is to ask yourself how you can afford to *miss* such opportunities!

Trade shows for similar products are common in nearly all types of manufacturing. Some focus on new machinery and equipment for producing the product; others focus on new products and/or new materials to manufacture current products. A manufacturer of plastic giftware items had ten employees. When the discard rate remained high in spite of close supervision, proper care of equipment and extra training for the injection molding machine operations, the owners began attending trade shows in hope of finding a solution. After some months and several trade shows, they learned of a new formula for plastic raw material that reduced the incidence of cracks and burns in products produced by injection molding. This discovery alone increased their profit margin by over eight percent.

Three brothers operated a company that sold several brands of copiers and also serviced them for their customers. The brother who did most of the servicing of machines found the same two or three types of problems occurring over and over in all brands of copiers they sold, regardless of how inexpensive or costly. In spite of his experience and training, he felt there must be something he was overlooking in his technical servicing or in teaching customers how to care for their machines—or both. In the past, although his brothers attended them on occasion, he had thought trade shows and conventions were mostly irrelevant to his work. When he finally attended a local trade show, he went from exhibit to exhibit asking about the problems he was facing. While there was no magical breakthrough, he picked up two pieces of information, one on servicing and another on a typical—but inappropriate—way people cleaned their machines. Both proved helpful in reducing the frequency of his problems. Because the firm did much of their servicing on a maintenance contract basis, more effective and less frequent service calls meant better use of his time and greater customer satisfaction.

Your Turn

Answer the following:

► List any trade journals and other periodicals that apply to your business.

► List any local or national business organizations to which you belong.

► List any trade shows or conventions available that apply to your business.

► Do you read the periodicals, attend organization meetings and/or go to the trade shows?

Worksheet: Keeping Informed About
New Products or Services

My Comparable Product or Service: _____

Date First Offered: _____

Unit Price (Item, Hour, etc.): _____

New Product or Service: _____

Firms that Make/Offer It	Date on Market	Unit Price	Description: Similarities to and Differences from Mine
1. _____ _____			
2. _____ _____			
3. _____ _____			
4. _____ _____			

ASK YOURSELF

▶ What is the importance, for your business, of monitoring suppliers, materials and services?

▶ Describe how you can control costs without sacrificing quality.

▶ How can you modify a current offering, drop a low-profit item or add to a present line to improve your product or service?

▶ Practically speaking, discuss some corrective action strategies for your company.

CHAPTER TWO

MANAGING YOUR BUSINESS OPERATIONS

DEVELOP STEP BY STEP BUSINESS SYSTEMS

Guiding Principle: Systematic business procedures are money in the bank. Lack of them is money down the drain.

Unless you are a born numbers cruncher, the chances are good that your product or service is the main focus of your attention and energy. After all, the reason you started your business is that you felt you had something special to offer, the know-how to produce it, and a group of potential clients waiting to buy it. Your secondary priority is likely to be marketing or other aspects of expanding the business. If it's on your list of priorities at all, establishing standard business procedures may well be a distant third—at least until you find yourself mired down in details, engaged in a never-ending struggle to keep up with financial records, embroiled in personnel disputes, or faced with the mind-boggling task of juggling finite time and energy to meet apparently infinite demands.

The good news is that establishing workable business routines, systems and procedures early on saves time, provides a method for tracking your financial progress as well as that all-important bottom line; it allows you to base the future of your business on sound knowledge, rather than on vague wishes or hopes. You will also discover that banks and other institutions or people in the business of lending money have a distinct tendency to look more favorably on firms that manage their business operations properly.

With this goal in mind then, this chapter deals with the day-to-day operations all business firms share in common:

▶ Make Customer Service Your Top Priority

▶ Revise—or Write!—Your Business Plan

▶ Handle Routine Financial Matters Systematically

▶ Establish Systems for Working with Employees, Outside Contractors and Suppliers

▶ Manage Time Efficiently

▶ Establish Systems for Maintaining Supply Levels and Equipment

CAUTION: While this chapter is concerned with the business side of your business, keep in mind that this book doesn't deal with any specific legal or tax requirements applicable to your particular business. Those requirements vary enormously from one locality to another and from one type of business to another; this book assumes that your business is up and running and you have already dealt with them.

MAKE CUSTOMER SERVICE YOUR TOP PRIORITY

One of the best known axioms in business is that you may have the best product or service available and offer it at the right price, but if you don't have customers, you don't have a business. Getting customers is a matter of marketing, advertising and, for many small businesses, referrals.

But unless you can make those customers happy and keep them happy, ultimately your business cannot match or outsell your competition well enough for you to stay in business. True customer service is based, first of all, on quality control over everything you offer. It also demands frequent monitoring of all procedures and systems you use to produce, sell and deliver your product or service. However, if you see your service obligations as ending with delivery, you are not providing genuine customer service, which begins in the initial stages of producing your product or service and ends well after delivery—if at all. True customer service requires careful targeting of customer needs and a consistent, firm commitment to serving those needs.

Company A, after selling several thousand units of a product, discovered a minor flaw in a part, overlooked during testing in the plant because it did not affect performance. Further testing, however, revealed that the defect could result in early failure of the unit. This company promptly manufactured new parts for all units sold and sent them to their customers, together with a letter of explanation and instructions for replacing the part. The letter also offered to pay each customer for the time spent replacing the part.

Company B, a small retail feed and pet supply store, initially stayed open six days a week. After a short time in business, they recognized that customer needs don't disappear on Sundays—they run out of feed or other necessary supplies, including some liniments and other over-the-counter pet medications—and began keeping the store open from 10:00 A.M. to 3:00 P.M. on Sundays.

In my own technical writing service firm, I realized after a few years in business that clients are often in such a hurry to get an operations manual or other document ready to use that, in spite of reviewing the rough draft, after the manual is completed they discover errors or omissions in procedures that need to be corrected. We began to make follow-up calls about six months after we delivered each manual, to inquire about the need for these changes and to offer to make the changes without additional cost—unless the client wants to add a whole section or other large chunk of information; in those instances, we charge a nominal fee to pay for the extra time required. While some clients don't avail themselves of this offer, all are invariably surprised and appreciative.

These examples illustrate real customer service as well as another point worth remembering: it's relatively simple to establish a customer service policy; it's not always easy to carry out that policy and maintain it over the long haul. But it's worth it. Companies who implement the policy build a large pool of goodwill whose worth cannot be calculated in dollars and cents.

Establish Specific Customer Service Policies and Procedures to Implement Them

Most companies of all sizes have a customer service policy and have every intention to follow through on that policy. Unfortunately, the road to failure is all too often paved with those good intentions. Why? A policy is one thing; translating that policy into action is something else. This is where clear, specific, detailed procedures are invaluable, even if you are the only one in direct contact with customers.

A common policy in manufacturing is the first-in, first-out principle—orders are filled in the order they are received. It's easy to establish this policy and tell everyone to follow it. But procedures on how to implement it are also necessary. Which comes first, for instance—an order dated the day before, which arrives today, or an order phoned in today? How are rush orders to be handled? And what about a repeat order of an item whose specifications are already on file, compared to an order for a new item? A set of clear, specific procedures will provide answers to these as well as other questions about this policy.

A wholesaler of cosmetics had a limited quantity of merchandise in a particular line available at a desirable price. Without thinking it through, the company sent out flyers to all customers who carried that line; they subsequently had to solve the problem of how to allocate 500 items among customer orders for 1,000. A procedure that spelled out details of which customers received what services first would have prevented the problem.

The prime commodity that service companies sell is time: for consulting, training or performing certain tasks. In this field, customer service procedures are invaluable for preventing or resolving conflicts in schedules. A firm that provided cleaning services for offices had ten employees; three were highly skilled, four were competent but not especially fast, and another three were new on the job. Also, predictably in this field, employee turnover was fairly high. After spending a good deal of time assigning people to clients' offices on a more or less random basis and getting quite a few customer complaints about the service, the owner worked out procedures that established priorities for the company's longtime customers, those with the largest offices, those with offices most and least difficult to clean, and those with equipment that required special care. While service complaints didn't disappear altogether, from then on they were fewer in number and the company found it much easier to make employee assignments.

Train Everyone Who Represents the Company in Customer Contact Procedures

Training sounds like a business operation only large companies need. But when it comes to customer service, every company must make sure everyone in contact with customers—office clerks, sales people, independent contractors, etc.—not only knows the policies and procedures for serving customers, but also has some training, however informal, in how to implement them. You would be surprised how quickly someone without such hands-on training can lose a customer or fail to gain a new one—especially when it is a matter of telephone contacts.

Recently, a telemarketer representing an office supplies company called a small company and reached the owner when he was meeting with a client. When the owner politely interrupted the telemarketer's initial pitch by saying he was very busy and would like to know what the caller was selling, the telemarketer snapped that he wasn't selling anything, he was just introducing people to the company. Clearly, that particular telemarketer would discourage anyone from becoming a customer of the company he represented, no matter how reliable that company might be. This instance illustrates how easy it is for someone without proper training to have a negative effect on your business—no matter how much time, thought and energy you have put into formulating policies and procedures for customer service.

Sales representatives for manufacturers are usually well trained in customer service, as it applies to selling. Just as typically, however, many are without training in after-sale follow-up customer service techniques. These can add another whole dimension to customer satisfaction and do much to assure repeat business. When a customer called to ask a question of the salesperson shortly after a large ticket piece of equipment was delivered, the salesperson's reply was a brusque, "I'm busy right now. Call the service department."

In contrast, the owner of a firm that manufactures a small line of office machines taught sales representatives to call each new customer about a week after the delivery of a new item to ask if there were questions or problems. When one customer replied, jokingly, that the machine worked fine, but the employee who operated it didn't, the sales person asked when it would be convenient to visit the office and take a few minutes to help the employee. After that visit, the customer made it a point to refer the manufacturer to others and, somewhat surprisingly, the employee who had received the help became an enthusiastic machine operator, proud of the new equipment and the "special" training!

A heating and air conditioning repair service that has to schedule appointments within a relatively large block of time routinely has its two clerks keep in contact with the repair staff by calling customers thirty to forty-five minutes before the truck arrives to tell them it's on its way. This soothes customers who may otherwise feel they've been forgotten, and cuts down on the number of frantic, repeat phone calls.

Keep Track of Customer Complaints

This is one area where small companies have an advantage. For large companies with many phones, clerks and perhaps multiple direct customer contacts, a record of customer complaints is often too complex or time consuming to be practical. For the small company with few phones and only one or two people who regularly contact the company's customers, such a record is both a feasible and valuable tool to monitor and improve customer service.

In its basic form, whoever deals with customers and takes calls uses a simple form to record the date and the nature of the complaint (the product doesn't work, the delivery is late, etc.). After you accumulate this information for a while, say a month or two, you have a picture of the number and types of complaints that your customers make. The intent of these tracking records is not to identify any customer or collect detailed information on specific problems or employees. Tracking this information regularly over a longer time allows you to detect significant changes in the pattern and/or number of such calls that point to certain trouble spots—among them, customer service.

A company that manufactured only one item, a child's safety belt for use in supermarket carts, had almost no complaints at first. When the number of complaints increased markedly, the owner contacted several of her larger local clients and dis- covered that the salesperson she had recently hired was not returning to each store to check on the installation of new belts. As a result, incorrectly installed belts were coming loose from their fastenings—a failure in customer service, not in the product itself.

A neighborhood delicatessen with a large business catering lunches for noontime business meetings began to receive more than a few complaints—some from customers of long standing. A few days of observation in the kitchen revealed that the extra packets of cream, butter, sugar, mayonnaise and catsup, previously sent with each order, were no longer being included. The problem, a new and over-zealous kitchen manager, had resulted in poor customer service. A ten minute "training" session with the new manager corrected the problem.

Your Turn

Answer the following:

► What aspects of customer service does your plan cover?

► Do your suppliers and/or employees know what your customer service policy is?

► List the specific procedures designed to implement your policy.

Worksheet: Monitoring Customer Complaints

Use or adapt this worksheet to keep track of the number and kinds of complaints you receive from customers about your products or services. Classify complaints as "late delivery," "wrong product," "doesn't work," "inferior materials," "poor quality of workmanship or service," etc.

Date	Firm or Person Who Complained	Product or Service	Nature of the Complaint

REVISE—OR WRITE!—YOUR BUSINESS PLAN

An informal survey I made among approximately seventy-five owners of businesses with one to ten employees or other staff revealed what I had expected. Only about 20 percent had a plan in written form; most of these were either incomplete—the authors having given up in despair—or consisted more of a statement of hopes and dreams than anything else. Of the remaining 80 percent, a few had never heard of a business plan, others didn't think it necessary to have one, and a few were quite frank in saying that they had been too busy getting started to spend weeks or months on some abstract document they considered to be of dubious value.

Yet, somebody out there thinks business plans are important. The market is awash with books on how to develop, write and even present business plans, presumably to gatherings of prospective financial backers. When I recently looked over current offerings at several large bookstores, I found a large crop of books—everything from comprehensive tomes weighing several pounds and dealing with every conceivable aspect of planning a new business of mega proportions, to more modest, concise volumes. The majority, regardless of size, used some rarified special language (*pro forma analysis,* for instance), and many got themselves mired down in intricate, highly detailed financial formulas and charts. No wonder so many small business owners don't have a plan.

This doesn't mean that a business plan is unnecessary or unimportant. On the contrary, without reasonable, clear, specific guidelines for present and future actions, sooner or later you will find yourself hip-deep in dilemmas, problems and questions for which you have no information and, consequently, no answers.

That's what happened to the owner of an appliance repair business who stumbled along an uncharted path for the first few years, relying on sheer luck and endless hours of work to make up for the fact that he didn't really know where his company was going or how to get there—even after he had developed a few dimly conceived goals. Finally, after one of his numerous calls for advice to the patient and extremely knowledgeable CPA who had handled the company's books from the beginning, the owner decided he had to organize the bits of paper covered with notes in a file folder labeled *Business Plan.* Out of this effort, which admittedly required hours of work, came a brief, ten-page prototype of the business plan his company uses today.

Regardless of what you have—incomplete, unrealistic or no plan at all—now is the time to rewrite or write a business plan that treats major aspects of your business. Base it on information in this book and, possibly, a book specifically on business plans. If you buy a book, and if you're not ready to plan a worldwide network of businesses, choose a concise one containing practical information, such as *Your New Business* by Charles L. Martin, Ph.D., published by Crisp Publications. That book provides a step-by-step approach to producing a plan. Make sure that whether you are revising one you already have or are starting from square one, your new business plan includes information on the topics in this chapter together with any others that are relevant to your business.

Establish Short and Long Range Goals and Objectives

This may seem too vague and general to be practical, but it isn't. If you have no ultimate goal (the aim or end you have in mind), it's like playing football without goalposts to signal touchdowns, or baking a cake without any idea of what kind of cake you want. To arrive at your broad goals, ask yourself questions along these lines, as well as other large questions that apply:

> ► *What size do you want your business to be?*
> As large as possible? Small enough so you can run it alone? Or . . . ?

> ► *What geographical area do you intend to cover?*
> Your neighborhood? Your city? Statewide? National? Multi-national?

> ► *How many products or services do you want to offer?*
> What you offer now? Do you want to add a few? Add many?

► *What kinds of products or services do you want to offer?*
What you produce now? Do you want to add a few related ones? Diversify considerably over time?

► *What other client/customer groups do you want to target?*
None? Different age groups? Special interest groups? Higher or lower financial level groups?

While goals and objectives are used interchangeably and may overlap, objectives are usually more specific; they deal with small segments and shorter time periods than goals. Under this definition, you might identify several objectives connected to a long-range goal of expanding, to cover additional geographical areas:

► *At what rate do you plan to expand into new territories?*
Expand slowly, by one locality or state at a time? By several branches at once? By franchising your product or service?

► *Which areas would be most likely to be successful?*
As much like your present area as possible? Urban? Rural? Smaller or larger populations? Labor pool available?

► *Which areas would have the greatest need for what you offer?*
Population that uses or could use what you sell? Age groups that need it most? Upper, middle, or lower income levels?

(Note: While this question and the preceding one may overlap, they are not the same; an area likely to buy a given item may not be the one with the greatest need for it.)

► *What will it cost?*
Rents? Services? Materials? Labor? Current economic outlook?

Keep in mind that these questions for formulating business plan goals and objectives are only samples. Your list may differ considerably. The question and answer approach, however, is an extremely productive means to identify and establish your goals and objectives.

Plan for Changes and Additions to Your Present Product(s) or Services

If you anticipate making changes in your present offerings—adding new products or services, eliminating low profit or outdated ones, making changes in what you produce now—it is essential to indicate them ahead of time in your business plan. Otherwise, you may find yourself behind your competition and without the necessary financial and other requirements when the time comes for change.

For most companies that manufacture products, planning ahead for change is crucial to success, since changes in current products and the addition of new products calls for preliminary changes in machines, tools and other plant equipment, as well as probable retraining or adding employees. All of this costs money, generally defined as capital outlay; this, in turn, requires advance planning that must be included in a practical business plan, preferably six months to several years before each change.

While the capital outlay for wholesale suppliers may not be as great as for manufacturers, adding a new line of food, cosmetics or gift items will cost money. For most wholesale firms, however small, it is also likely to require more space for storing the new items. The cost of adding new products may not be as great for wholesalers as for retailers, but other costs, including advertising, are likely to be substantial enough to warrant inclusion in a business plan.

For consulting and other professional services, adding a new service often involves hiring someone with the necessary training and experience. When the new service is included in a business plan, the owner of the company can be on the lookout for a person who might later fill a new position. For other kinds of service companies, adding new services can require planning of a different kind. The owner of a local auto repair shop had a really brief business plan consisting of notes on possible expansion of service and a few rough figures estimating costs and other necessities. After five years in business, when the owner decided he was ready to offer brake repair as well as his regular tune-up and engine repair, he discovered that he had no space left in his present quarters. A more detailed plan, with estimates of space requirements as well as costs, would have made it possible for him to add the new service a year earlier than he did.

Identify Potential New Markets or Target Groups for Your Products or Services

This is among the most important information to include in your business plan, because it is one of the basic ways to expand a small company without incurring the sometimes prohibitive costs of adding to your offerings. It also functions as a hedge against economic recessions or seasonal fluctuations in the amount of business you do. Expanding your market and, thereby, your potential client base, calls for creative thought and ingenuity; time spent now thinking it through on paper may increase your profits and reduce the lean times if your business is cyclical.

A woman who designed and made small ceramic figurines to sell to retailers in a popular tourist area of Southern California found herself caught in seasonal fluctuations that provided excellent profits about half the year, and very small profits the rest of the time. While she had a business plan that covered most aspects of her business, it didn't include anything on developing new markets; she thought she had already targeted the available local market and didn't want to expand beyond that area. One day a friend commented that some of the figurines "could be anyone," when she saw some before they were painted and glazed. At that point, the owner realized she could expand her line and her market significantly by making minor changes in some designs and colors to appeal to children—a market she had not reached before and one that reduced significantly the seasonal aspect of her business.

A firm that designed and taught business writing workshops to the employees of large companies developed a business plan after being in a business about four years. While writing their plan, the two owners realized they could expand their client base by developing materials to teach another group— employees who had considerable job skills but for whom

English was a second language. With this expansion, their business increased over forty percent within a year.

Visualize New Marketing and Advertising Strategies

This part of a business plan is important for keeping up with changes in your own product or service, applicable developments in technology and changes in available markets. Questions to ask yourself as you consider possible shifts in your marketing and advertising strategies might well be the following, among others:

▶ What changes in product or service have you made that might call for additional or different marketing and advertising?

▶ If you have expanded since your start-up, how could you extend the area or frequency of advertising?

▶ What are some new target groups you might be able to reach?

▶ What other advertising media might be cost-effective, practical and profitable?

▶ What technology developments might make it desirable or mandatory to adjust your strategies?

▶ What former markets might have disappeared, or what new ones might have opened up for your product or service?

Establish or Revise Present Business Systems

Every business plan needs to allow for changes in operating systems to keep them efficient, current and adequate for meeting your business requirements. What worked well at the beginning may eventually be cumbersome, time consuming and therefore inefficient for your present volume and type of business.

The basic approach is to ask yourself how you can improve on the following:

- ▶ Office or plant work space arrangements

- ▶ Project scheduling

- ▶ Payroll and other financial procedures

- ▶ Storage and accessibility of office and other materials

- ▶ Office or plant equipment

If questions like these are incorporated into your business plan, you automatically ensure a periodic review of the systems necessary to run your business efficiently.

One change that we made in our work space after about five years improved traffic flow and also provided extra, much needed storage space. We had five bookcases lined up along one wall in our front office. This didn't leave much space for a desk and phones between the bookcases and the front door. One day we moved them so that they formed a right angle on the other side of that office; the change left plenty of space for the desk and created another storage area behind the bookcases. While our business plan didn't include anything as specific as how to move furniture, it did contain a question about making office work space more efficient. Ultimately, this led to the change.

Specify Customer Service Policy and Procedures

Frequent examination of your customer service policy and procedures will make sure that they continue to operate smoothly, that they are implemented properly, and that your customers are receiving the kind of service that will keep them with you over a long period of time. To accomplish these objectives, your business plan must specify a review of policy at stated intervals, as well as periodic examination of all procedures that have a bearing on how well you are serving your customers. If applicable to your business, the plan should also provide for either continuous or periodic feedback from your customers, preferably conducted by you, another management person and, possibly, by your sales people. To simplify the procedure, the plan may even include a customer feedback form or checklist.

Include Detailed Financial Information and Projections

Some books on preparing business plans seem to put undue emphasis on financial data. Such information, necessary for all business plans, is critical to plans for small businesses whose fluctuating cash flow frequently causes anxiety. If your business is relatively new and you do not have a business plan, you need to consult with an accountant and/or get a book on preparing business plans. Make sure your plan contains financial information on the following: keeping track of your financial status, making reasonably sound short-range projections by the quarter and by the year, and making long-range, three-year and five-year projections. Businesses differ
on how much of what financial data a workable business plan will include, but most should cover the following topics, at least:

► Funding sources and needs for new and replacement purchases, cash flow shortages and expansion

► Break even point (the point at which total fixed and variable costs equal your income)

► Cash flow over stated periods of time

► Balance sheets (profit and loss statements)

► Financial statements with data on equipment depreciation

► Quarterly, six-month, annual, 3-year and/or 5-year projections for the above topics, as applicable

► Ongoing records on fixed and variable costs

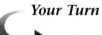

Your Turn   *Answer the following:*

- ► Do you have a business plan?

- ► List your top five short term goals.

- ► List your top five long term goals.

- ► List some potential new markets for your business.

HANDLE ROUTINE FINANCIAL MATTERS SYSTEMATICALLY

The key word here is *systematically.* Everyone who runs a business keeps financial records of some kind. Unless you develop a system for maintaining them on a reasonably regular basis, it can be a burdensome, confusing task. At the very least, systematic records reduce the number and frequency of end-of-the-month panics and tax time nightmares.

If you are the sole owner of your business, it's unfortunately far too easy to let record keeping slide, under the pressures of keeping up with other demands on your time.

If your company is a partnership, record keeping can be divided, but if one partner maintains proper records and the other doesn't, not only is discord between the partners probable, the records may not be accurate. If your company is a corporation, legal requirements make good records mandatory, since penalties for procrastination and error tend to be swift and severe.

Regardless of your company's organizational structure, performing routine financial business tasks will be easier and seem less intrusive if you use two approaches to the work: divide the tasks into categories, and schedule time for each category in advance. Ultimately, you may establish and organize categories according to a system of your own. Meanwhile, the five financial categories in this chapter identify tasks that are both necessary and practical for most types of business: cash flow (routine bills, invoices, purchases and checkbook balancing), taxes, payroll, operating costs and profits, and contingency funds.

Cash Flow: Pay Bills, Send Invoices to Clients, Make Necessary Purchases, and Balance the Company Checkbook

This sounds like a lot for one category, but since they are related, it is easier to deal with them together. If at all possible, schedule a time when there are no distractions, preferably on one or two weekends a month; if weekends are your business times, select another time slot.

A manufacturer may need to do this, or have a clerk do most of it, only once a month. A retail sales firm will have to total receipts on a daily basis, of course, but can probably handle the other items in this category on a weekly, biweekly or monthly basis. Many owners routinely work at least two Saturdays a month for two to four hours, although it is occasionally necessary to order materials or send invoices at other times. The time required for handling these financial duties will differ from one company to another, but a schedule can help enormously.

Figure and/or Pay Taxes

For this category, I have a strong recommendation. If you are a math genius who knows all the tax requirements for your particular business, establish a regular schedule for dealing with sales taxes, payroll taxes, quarterly estimates and local, state and federal annual taxes—whatever is applicable to your company. If you aren't a financial wizard, *use a qualified business accountant,* preferably a CPA and preferably one who specializes in handling small business clients.

By sheer luck and a friend's recommendation, when I first started my company I made contact with a CPA small business specialist who has handled my books ever since. His services aren't cheap, but his work, advice and willingness to help whenever I have had a question have more than paid for his services over the years. Furthermore, because I don't have to spend time figuring and worrying about taxes and quarterly and annual financial statements, I can concentrate my time and energy on running and developing my business.

Make Out the Payroll

In some small businesses, this presents little difficulty, especially if you have only yourself and one or two employees, and if you have an accountant who keeps you informed of the correct deductions for SDI, FICA, and income taxes. In the interest of time and accuracy, if you need to process a payroll for a number of employees, I strongly recommend that you use an accountant or a payroll service. Assuming that you have been running your own business for a year or more, you already know that the demands on your time and energy are heavy. Why add to the burden when others can shoulder this part of it?

Figure Your Operating Costs and Profits

Large companies have employees and sometimes entire departments to keep this and related financial data. Small business owners have to, and should, keep these records themselves, at least once every six months and possibly every quarter, depending on the nature and volume of your business. No single other type of record can yield a better picture of where you are and how you are doing than the exact figures for a recent time period on costs and gross and net profits, according to your break-even point—where your total fixed and standard regular costs match your gross income. If your income is below this point, you're losing money; above it, you are making a profit.

These figures can help you in other ways as well. If your business is seasonal or otherwise cyclical, you can see more clearly when and where to cut or increase spending for materials or labor. You may be better able to determine when more or different marketing and advertising is advisable, when your prices need adjustment, and whether production rates and schedules are in line with your present volume of business. If your business volume remains fairly stable throughout the year, you can use these figures to make estimates for the short-term future and use the estimates to allocate money for taxes and other necessities.

Establish or Maintain Your Contingency Fund

Chapter 1 discusses the value of having a contingency fund for unexpected expenses as one of several corrective action strategies. If you don't have an emergency fund, establish it as soon as possible; maintain the records on it as a specific category of routine financial matters. Handling it as a regular part of your financial work assures you of having a separate sum of money available when it's needed.

Your Turn

Answer the following:

► How much time do you spend handling routine financial matters?

► What are your usual operating costs?

► What is your usual profit?

Worksheet: Tracking Quarterly Costs and Profits

For the greatest accuracy, make sure that you list the income earned and costs incurred within each quarter, even when you receive payments and pay for costs in a late quarter.

Time Period	Gross Income	Fixed Costs	Variable Costs	Net Income or Loss (–)
YEAR: _____ QUARTER: 1st				
2nd				
3rd				
4th				
YEAR: _____ QUARTER: 1st				
2nd				
3rd				
4th				
YEAR: _____ QUARTER: 1st				
2nd				
3rd				
4th				

ESTABLISH SYSTEMS FOR WORKING WITH EMPLOYEES, OUTSIDE CONTRACTORS AND SUPPLIERS

Why in the world do you need a system for working with employees and other people who do work for you? Yes, you need to know how to approach potential clients, get them to buy from you and to become regular customers. But special techniques surely aren't necessary for those who work for you. You tell them what you want done, they do it and you pay them. Right? Wrong. Unfortunately, however, a considerable number of managers, plant supervisors and top executives don't realize that people skills apply at least as much to staff as they do to clients. If you establish a set of working procedures and, where necessary, policies for dealing with people, your company will run much more smoothly than if you handle each situation as it appears or operate by what is sometimes referred to as *management by knee-jerk reaction.*

As a small business owner, you probably don't think of yourself as an executive in charge of departments or large numbers of people. Yet, small businesses typically make use of many outside services to support their in-house or in-plant operations. Take a minute to make a mental count of the people who repair equipment, provide special services such as word processing, accounting or billing, furnish supplies and provide labor for special projects on a temporary basis or as subcontractors. Quite a number, aren't there? Perhaps more than you thought? A few relatively informal systems for handling basic relationships and people situations can save you a good deal of worry, sleepless nights and, quite possibly, an unpleasant legal entanglement or two.

Establish a Network of Local Suppliers and Subcontractors for Essential Support Services

When you want someone to put information on a special software program, for example—your new business plan perhaps?—and money is in short supply, it's tempting to make a few calls and select whoever seems able to do it for the best price. Sometimes that works out fine, but not always. If, over the years, you have established a network of local people who provide services and materials you need, you can be confident about the results and in the long run save time and money. You know what to expect, the providers know what you want, and when special situations arise, such as the need for swift service, you are much more likely to get prompt service than if you habitually jump from one provider to another.

Companies differ in what outside services they use, of course. Manufacturers require raw materials, wholesale and retail sales firms may rely on a great many suppliers, and service companies often use outside contractors for work projects. But a few basic policies and procedures apply to all:

1. If the price for something is higher than you can afford, say so; offer to refer the provider to others and use the services regularly in return for a lower price.

2. Pay your suppliers promptly. Their business is probably smaller than yours and, besides, you'll find yourself on the receiving end of the best possible services when you have a reputation for reliability.

3. If something they do or provide is wrong, say so without anger. Everyone makes mistakes; most of them are honest errors. You've made one or two yourself, haven't you?

4. When you ask for some service or item that is out of the ordinary, take great care to explain exactly what you want. Encourage the provider to ask questions when necessary.

5. Compliment suppliers when they produce particularly good work or complete a rush job on time. Give bonuses for outstanding performance or service. Compliments don't have to be extravagant and bonuses don't have to be large; both let those who provide support services know that you recognize and appreciate their efforts. The warm glow they feel lasts a long time and does much to assure you of a continuing good working relationship.

Don't dismiss the importance of these ideas; you can probably even add a few of your own. They're deceptively simple—so easy that too many people overlook them as unnecessary, although they incorporate basic approaches for working successfully with others.

Make Sure That Employees and Suppliers Know and Follow Your Requirements and Procedures for Each Task

It is vital to provide direction and training for people who work for you. Large companies often have an entire training department. Small ones seldom have even the basic elements of a training program; if cost effective, training programs can prove to be a valuable tool.

For manufacturers, training and operations manuals reduce both the time spent in training new employees or suppliers and the number of errors they make, thereby lowering costs. But what about a retail store with one or two employees? In a simpler form, the same principle applies. You don't have to be a skilled writer to put down, perhaps on two or three pages, *exactly* what tasks are necessary to perform each job. For a new stock clerk or general helper, the job description might describe unloading cartons of merchandise from delivery trucks two days a week, checking and restocking store shelves as needed, and cleaning all floors and counters before opening time and again after the store closes. For a supplier, the same few pages might contain information about when and where deliveries are to be made, the procedures for checking off each delivery, and the procedure to follow if an item must be back-ordered.

Whatever system you establish, it is best to put all requirements and tasks involved in each job in writing, and have employees sign the written sheet or sheets. In this way, there will be no misunderstandings later. You may not think of these guidelines as training in the usual sense. But when you use simple directive procedures, they do, indeed, train people in what you expect them to do and how they are to do it. You will discover that written procedures have two significant advantages; they save time and reduce errors—both result in greater efficiency.

Correct Problems Connected to Staff or Suppliers Promptly

The central key to a workable system is promptness. The longer you delay action when someone does not produce what you expect or has a disruptive effect on others in the company, the harder it is to act effectively. Every book on management and every seminar on personnel problems will emphasize this. However, it is sometimes difficult for the operator of a small business to put the principle into effect.

The new, untrained office manager of a small finance company provides an example of how not to do this. She was in charge of the five clerks. One was a young woman only a few years younger than the manager, who arrived late to work two or three days a week. Since that clerk was also the most accurate and productive of the five employees, the manager ignored the problem until she realized that this clerk's tardiness was having a negative effect on office morale. Then and only then, the manager tried to correct the problem, first by talking to the clerk. Later, since the manager passed near the clerk's home on her way to work, she stopped to pick her up. The effect of the latter effort was to make the manager late to work, too. Ultimately, having learned her first hard lesson in people management, the manager had to fire the clerk. The manager learned two things from that experience: correct such problems as soon as they appear; the line between supervisor and friend must be maintained for management to be effective.

While personnel problems take a variety of forms, the same types of problems appear in manufacturing, sales and service companies. The following list of step-by-step procedures can be useful in setting up your own system for correcting the people problems you encounter most often:

1. In small businesses, it is easy to become too friendly with employees or providers you use regularly. Avoid this trap.

2. When a problem surfaces, correct it PROMPTLY.

3. Explain the problem clearly, in as much detail as you can, and in as objective and neutral a tone as possible. Avoid sounding either angry or friendly. Maintain your objectivity; this helps to keep the focus on the problem and not on your attitude towards the person.

4. Ask the person the reason for the problem and LISTEN to the answer, however off the wall it may sound.

5. Respond briefly to the explanation. Then ask the person what he or she thinks would solve the problem. Again, LISTEN. No matter how ineffective or irrelevant the offered solution may be, you will begin to perceive something about the person and perhaps about the problem itself.

6. Do not allow yourself to be drawn into a discussion of what other people do, or how someone else is to blame. Point out that the problem belongs to the person you are talking to and the purpose of the session is to correct the problem, not to place blame elsewhere.

7. For an employee, suggest a course of action and a due date. Frequently, additional training or retraining for part of the person's work can be effective. Sometimes, reassignment to another, more suitable job will work; other times, rescheduling a project or task in some way can help.

8. For an outside supplier or subcontractor, explain what you expect to continue using the person's services.

9. After an appropriate interval, follow up on the discussion. Whether the person is an employee or outside provider, ask if there are any problems in getting the problem solved; if it is solved or if improvement is noticeable, make sure you comment favorably about it. If there is no visible improvement, reiterate that the problem is real and must be corrected.

10. If none of the above works, you will have to let the person know that a parting of the ways is imminent

unless correction is prompt. Then, fire the employee according to company policies, or discontinue using the services of an outside provider or contractor.

It isn't easy or pleasant to deal with people problems. For one of my contract writers who I believe should do a better job in less time at this point, I have just completed step 7 by having an outside expert, a colleague of mine, provide extra training in certain information gathering and writing techniques. I'm not looking forward to proceeding to step 8, but it may be necessary. If so, I'll make clear what the conditions are for future assignments; if the writer improves, I'll be grateful for salvaging the services of someone who has the basic skills my company needs.

 Your Turn

Answer the following:

► List dependable suppliers of your goods and services.

► What is your system for solving "people" problems?

► What are your requirements for supplying your goods and services?

Worksheet: Checklist for Establishing Schedules and Time Lines

CLIENT/CUSTOMER: _____

PRODUCT OR SERVICE TO BE SCHEDULED: _____

1. What is the project's priority?

   ☐ 1(top)　　　☐ 2　　　☐ 3　　　☐ 4　　　☐ 5 (bottom)

2. What is my *tentative* time line for the entire project:

   Start date: _____　　　Finish date: _____

3. What are the material and labor requirements?

   Materials (Kinds? Quantity?): _____

   _____

   Labor (How many? What skills?): _____

   _____

4. What are my sources/suppliers for materials and labor: _____

   _____

5. What is my *adjusted* time line for the entire project?

   Start date: _____　　　Finish date: _____

6. What problems are likely to appear during the project? _____

   _____

7. What is my *final* time line for the entire project?

   Start date: _____　　　Finish date: _____

8. When did I/we actually complete this project?

   Actual finish date: _____

MANAGE TIME EFFICIENTLY

This is undoubtedly one of the most difficult tasks for people in business. As a small business owner, it can be overwhelming; there are so many demands on your time and energy that at times you inevitably have to steal time from one urgent task to spend on another equally urgent one. I wish I had a magic formula for managing time. If I did, I wouldn't be here in the office at 10:00 o'clock at night, writing this book. But here I am, lengthening my work day to handle the multitude of tasks confronting me—a common method of time management for small business owners, especially those whose work, like mine, runs in cycles with frequent, exceedingly tight deadlines.

Despite the above disclaimer, there are some practical techniques for achieving greater efficiency in the use of time—relatively simple ways to organize materials, projects and schedules to make them manageable, or certainly more manageable than they may be at present. Nowhere is it more evident than in small business that time is money. Most small business owners work long, hard hours. They deserve all the help they can get. Even if it is a matter of shaving only small amounts of time from various tasks, the cumulative effect will be valuable. Another advantage is that when you are aware of time, you use it more effectively and are much less apt to overlook or wait too long to begin a given task or project.

Arrange Projects According to Priority

Every book on management skills and every seminar on how to work more efficiently recommends organizing your tasks according to their priority. Sometimes this advice comes with forms to help you identify and list items as A (top), B (middle) and C (third) in importance. Many small business owners have read and heard about such techniques a hundred times before they really sink in; even then, some consider them seriously only when they are buried under a horrendous work load and the schedule for getting it done is impossible.

The owner of an appliance repair business began to try to manage his time by making a form with lines and the three categories mentioned above. At the end of the week he could no longer follow the cross-outs, arrows and other desperate reorganizing attempts; he discarded the form and started over, this time setting up a project folder with index tabs. It was approximately two months before he knew that system was too cumbersome; it took too much time just to shift tabs for each new project, to keep them in alphabetical order. However, he still felt the idea ought to work. It did, too. As soon as he began jotting down tasks for the week or day at the top of an $8\frac{1}{2} \times 11$ inch pad of paper he kept on his desk for making notes, recording phone numbers, and other similar temporary data, he had a convenient, quick reminder right under his eyes when he needed it most, usually when a customer called with an urgent job. He makes changes when necessary, especially in the daily list, by simply crossing out an item and writing another one in its place—often when he is stuck waiting on the phone and can't do other kinds of work anyway.

Simplicity, informality and flexibility turned out to be the keys for him, but I suspected that his system would drive some people crazy. I polled a number of other small business owners to find out how they establish workable priority systems. I discovered a variety of systems that differed widely in their form, but had two basic characteristics in common. *Flexibility* was one; all lists of priorities could be changed swiftly to fit changing circumstances. *Convenient location* was the other; in one way or another, every workable arrangement was located where the user could get at it quickly.

A floor supervisor in a plant, whose primary job is to schedule incoming orders and assign them to operators and machines, keeps an oversize clipboard hanging on a hook at one side of his desk, at a convenient height for writing standing up. At one side of the clipboard is a black pen; at the other side, a red one. The clipboard holds several sheets of 11 × 14 inch wide-lined paper with the following typed headings: *Order #, In Date, Operator/Machine, Due Date,* and *Date Completed.* He marks all regular orders in black and marks all rush orders in red.

Most of the systems salespeople use are scheduled by location within a sales territory, as well as by priority. One of the best uses 4 × 6 inch index cards in four colors, one color for each part of the territory: north, south, east and west. Each lined card has a space at the top for the customer or contact's name. Below are five column headings: *Date, Regular, New, Small* and *Large.* Under each heading, the salesperson makes check marks to indicate whether the contact is a regular customer or a new contact, and whether the company is small or large. After writing in the company and contact person's name at the top on cards of the appropriate location color, the salesperson first sorts them by color and then makes check marks under the headings where information is available. After each day's sales calls, the cards contain basic information necessary for future scheduling and priority. The color coding for location simplifies scheduling; the headings help to arrange cards in an approximate order of priority.

According to my informal survey, professional consultants, including two who hold seminars on time management, tend to carry around a scheduling/calendar/phone number organizing book. Most books bulge with bits of extra paper; many bristle with little pop-up quick stick tabs in various colors, which usually indicate either time or importance priorities. The one I thought especially good, uses a vinyl covered $8\frac{1}{2} \times 11\frac{1}{2}$ inch portfolio with two inside pockets, one on each side. In the left pocket is a calendar with one month on each page; this is for appointment times and dates, with the most important ones in green. In the right pocket is another similar calendar, with colored lines running across the dates, some showing three day periods and other indicating a week or more. Each color indicates a different seminar topic: blue for ones on time management, red for those on supervisory skills, and so on. With this system, the user can avoid conflicts in time and schedule new seminars by glancing quickly at both sides of the portfolio.

Regardless of the system for establishing priorities, nearly all of the ones that work best are informal as well as simple; most are systems the users have devised for themselves, a point to keep in mind when you are trying to manage your time more efficiently.

Establish Time Lines for Completing Projects

For some tasks and projects, the time line is built in from the start. Orders for raw materials, stock and completed items must be delivered by a certain date. Services must be performed at stated times or completed on a certain date. For these, what is crucial is setting the order date or start date far enough in advance to be reasonably sure the order or project will be ready on time. Since there are often a number a variables connected to availability of materials, labor and working time, this isn't easy for any business, although it may be somewhat more manageable for small businesses whose owners direct all or most business operations.

After you have been in business for a while, you will have an idea of how much time is required to complete your projects. Use this information to establish your tentative time line or deadline for completing each type of work. Then, take time to determine the labor and material requirements, where appropriate, and adjust your preliminary time line according to their availability.

At that point, you're finished, right? Wrong. Among the other matters to consider before your time line is properly established, you need to identify possible glitches and build in extra time to compensate for them. Glitches come in many shapes and sizes, ranging from a raw material that is always in short supply, through production conflicts and breakdowns, to the availability of labor during the flu season. And just when you think you have faced every possible impediment to getting a job done, another one, totally new and unexpected, will appear. Trust me.

Now that you've allowed extra time for the inevitable problems, have you finally established a firm time line? Not yet. Now is the time to add a safety margin of extra time, as much as you can afford within the time you have available. It's easy to omit this last step in scheduling, particularly when your business is quite new and you are anxious to get and complete as much work as you can. After more than ten years in business, I still catch myself on the brink of promising a document to a client within an unrealistic time frame. What I try to do, given a finite amount of available time, is skip the safety margin for my old clients and push their manuals through as swiftly as possible. For new orders, I force myself to provide enough lead time to prevent late delivery. With experience, you will find it easier to establish proper time lines for your own business.

Monitor Time Lines and Work Schedules Regularly

It would be nice to think that you can relax once project time lines are properly established, your suppliers know when they have to deliver materials and services, and whoever is in charge of a given project knows exactly what to do and when to do it. It doesn't work that way, though. Suppliers are late with a delivery and for unknown reasons, that information doesn't reach you for two days. The baker who starts baking the day's supply of bread at 3:00 A.M. twists an ankle and in the ensuing crisis, another is born when you are not informed of this accident until 7:00 A.M. Your most reliable seminar trainer leaves the entire day's set of workshop materials at home, thirty miles from the work site. And on and on.

These are small examples that you can probably multiply several times over for your own business. The question here is how to monitor the work in process well enough to prevent such stumbling blocks from occurring. The answer, of course, it that you can't prevent them. What you can do is reduce their frequency by incorporating monitoring systems into your customary procedures.

Consider the above examples. An in-house extension phone on the dock, a live clerk or answering machine at the other end, and clear instructions to Receiving to report any missing items from any order at any time of the day or night will minimize and maybe eliminate future two-day delays in reporting. The phone and the instructions work together as a monitoring device. A similar system would work for the bakery if a reporting phone number were posted in large print above the kitchen phone, and all employees on all shifts had instructions to call that number if anything interfered with production when the bakery was closed.

As for the third example, the trainer who left the materials at home, you probably couldn't do much to prevent the problem, except to provide checklists for all sessions, and instruct trainers to always go over them just before leaving for the work site. The training coordinator who faced this problem happened to be on-site, sitting in on some of the six sessions the company was running that day. While the trainer called her mother and asked her to bring the materials, the coordinator took over the session, explained the situation briefly, and conducted an informal review question and answer session before the materials arrived. Sheer luck? Partly, but the coordinator was on-site that day for the express purpose of monitoring the three trainers who were running the workshops; she could conduct the review session because she was thoroughly familiar with the workshop materials. Monitoring, then, is not a guarantee that such accidents won't happen, but it is certainly worth examining your own operations to see where and how you can put monitoring systems in place.

Your Turn   *Answer the following:*

➤ What tasks create gridlock in your business?

➤ How can you avoid this problem?

➤ List your projects in order of priority.

➤ What is your timeline for completing projects?

ESTABLISH SYSTEMS FOR MAINTAINING SUPPLY LEVELS AND EQUIPMENT

It would be great if there were a perfect system for handling the multitude of details necessary to maintain office and plant routine operations. While some computer programs can help companies keep track of inventory, and there are many kinds of periodic and continuous inventory procedures, no one has yet devised a system that eliminates the need for someone to make sure there is enough copy paper and sufficient paper towels or wipe rags on hand before a new supply arrives. In large firms, office managers, plant supervisors and maintenance departments take care of most of these necessities.

In smaller firms, where the person who checks on supplies is likely to be you, setting up systematic procedures will significantly reduce the number of times that you or a wild-eyed employee makes a frantic search for the supply of No. 10 gizmos. Schedules for checking office and/or plant supplies, buying in larger, cost effective quantities and maintaining equipment properly will also reduce your blood pressure, lessen the chances of falling behind schedule on projects, and permit you to focus your attention on more satisfying and profitable pursuits.

Establish a Schedule for Checking Office and Plant Supplies

After your business has been in operation several months or years and the demand for ordinary supplies has stabilized, you can make a close estimate of how much of what you usually need and how often you have to place orders. To arrive at that point, however, it's useful to establish a system and a schedule. Checklists work very well, especially if your lists are categorized according to location, type and typical rates of use, with columns for date and quantity of last order, amount or number of packages on hand, and quantity to order next time. In very small offices it is probably quite easy to glance through supply shelves to see how many boxes of paper clips and pens there are; even in these instances, the number and variety of supplies can be more easily tracked with a simple checklist.

Scheduling orders at specific intervals eliminates the need for frequent orders that interrupt the regular flow of work and can require a surprising amount of extra time—to fill out order blanks, make phone calls, sign for deliveries and the like. Once your system is in place, you may have to order routine supplies only once or twice a quarter or even less often. Just make sure your supply orders are scheduled well in advance of need.

Buy in Cost Effective Quantities

Storage space is usually limited in small businesses; within those limitations, always look for the quantity purchase price breaks. One company, for instance uses vast amounts of paper, in large rolls that take up considerable space. But the price breaks for purchasing in quantity made it worthwhile to expand the storage space for paper and allot less space for other, less expensive and less frequently needed items. Dashing out to the local stationery store or other retail supplier to buy a pen or some other similar item wastes time and money. One ordinary roller point pen usually costs anywhere between eighty cents and a dollar. One box of twelve pens usually drops the price to about fifty-five cents each; two or three dozen at a time can drop the price to forty-five cents each.

This may sound like nickel and dime stuff; in a way, it is. But unless your company cash flow is dangerously low, this type of quantity purchasing saves significant amounts of money over a period of time and represents a genuine saving for small companies who need every penny. Quantity purchasing on a fairly regular schedule also saves the extra time you'd otherwise spend in placing more frequent orders, writing more checks and making desperate forays out to find some necessary item.

Establish Systems for Maintaining Equipment and Office or Plant Facilities

Annual maintenance agreements for expensive equipment and/or machinery is a must for the first several years—at least until depreciation makes the cost of such agreements greater than the value of the equipment. While the temptation is sometimes great to save the expense of a maintenance agreement, the result can all too often be a machine that eventually requires expensive repair or replacement because it wasn't properly maintained on a regular basis. Fax machines make an excellent case in point. While they are working, they function very well; when something goes wrong, it can be a tedious, time-consuming and expensive matter to get the problem corrected.

A few years ago, my company, which sends and receives review drafts of the manuals we write, invested in a plain paper fax machine with a number of bells and whistles. We also purchased a maintenance agreement at a cost of $335 a year. There were no problems for the first two years. Then, the machine began throwing tantrums every time we tried to send anything over one or two pages. On occasion, it refused to receive transmissions. Three service calls, each approximately two hours long, fixed the problem—for a while. Then it decided to start yelling at us to *check the paper, check the paper,* although there was plenty of paper available. This time, it took only two service calls before it functioned normally again— calls that required four and a half hours of on-site service and replacement of a number of parts. At $100 an hour, the time charge would have totaled $950; according to the technician, the parts would have cost another $200. The math was clearly in our favor. The total repair costs would have been $1,150; the cost of the maintenance agreement over a two year period was $670. While not a huge sum, the savings of $470 wasn't parking meter change.

Similarly, it is less costly in the long run to purchase cleaning, trash removal and special waste disposal services, where applicable, on a contract basis that spells out exactly what is to be done, how it is to be done, and how frequently the service is to be performed. Nothing is perfect, of course, and you will have to spend some time monitoring and correcting problems with these services. But for the most part, they remove another source of worry and save you money. Peace of mind for a small business owner means a lot!

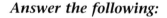

Your Turn

Answer the following:

► List the basic supplies and equipment that are critical to the smooth operation of your business.

► What checking, purchasing or maintenance schedules do you have in place?

► What is your schedule for checking office and plant supplies?

ASK YOURSELF

▶ In your business, which of the six ordinary business operations listed below are working well? Discuss what makes each work well.

▶ Which of the six are OK, but would benefit from some improvements or modifications? Describe how each could be improved or modified.

▶ Which are weak or missing altogether? What plans do you have to change this?

▶ Which one should you establish or improve right away? How and when will you do so?

- Customer Service System

- Business Plan

- Routine Financial Matters

- Working with People

- Time Management

- Maintenance Systems

SURVIVING COMMON PITFALLS, PRATFALLS AND MAJOR DISASTERS

MINIMIZE OR PREVENT OBSTACLES

Guiding Principle: Forewarned is forearmed! Advance notice can minimize or prevent common obstacles.

People who believe it's possible to achieve a smooth, trouble-free operation are from another planet. Glitches and major problems are bound to occur, sometimes with discouraging regularity. But that doesn't mean you have to sit with your hands folded, waiting for trouble to loom over the horizon. There are excellent strategies to help you avoid, surmount and survive obstacles that plague small businesses. Applying preventive or corrective measures reduces the number of boulders in your path, and gives you a sense of satisfaction at meeting challenges. In the long run, overcoming such problems can even make your business stronger and more competitive.

You have to take prompt corrective action or get around PITFALLS—problems you can't foresee and therefore can't prevent—with diversionary tactics. You can apply foresight and advance planning to prevent many PRATFALLS—errors of judgment and other similar mistakes—before they happen. You can survive MAJOR DISASTERS—fires, floods, earthquakes, riots, war, personal illness or injury and other events over which you have no control—by recognizing their cataclysmic character and making advance preparations to help your business surmount them.

In this chapter, the focus is on raising your level of awareness about certain obstacles, and how you can significantly increase the chances that your business will survive them. You will learn how to:

► Compensate for Pitfalls

► Prevent Typical Pratfalls

► Prepare for Major Disasters

COMPENSATE FOR PITFALLS

Pitfalls, those unanticipated problems that lurk around the next bend in the road, just when it looks like smooth sailing ahead, come in all sizes, shapes and degrees. Generally, they fall into one of two classifications: internal or external. *Internal* pitfalls, common to all types of business, are likely to stem from either of two attitudes on the part of the owner: neglect of some aspect of the business because of time or other pressures, or complacency based on the belief that some well established routine or system will continue to function properly. *External* pitfalls, common in some types of business and almost nonexistent in others, usually stem from technological advances or changes in outside conditions and competition.

The first two topics in this chapter deal with internal pitfalls; the next two discuss external ones. Owners who develop a high level of awareness can sometimes prevent internal pitfalls and certainly will be able to apply corrective action measures far more promptly than those who have not learned to expect the unexpected. Owners of businesses prone to external pitfalls will develop the habits of good drivers: keeping a lookout on both sides and the rear, while focusing on the road ahead.

Don't Neglect Any Aspect of Your Business

Because businesses vary in their requirements, the amount of time and attention you need to give to your product or service, routine business operations marketing and advertising will also vary at times. A manufacturing firm may require greater attention to the product, a retail sales company may have to spend more time on daily operations, and a service company may require more focus on marketing techniques. Also, depending on the nature of your business, you may have to focus primarily on one aspect at certain times and/or certain stages in the development of your company.

In spite of these differences, however, it's vital to keep in mind that, with few exceptions, over the long haul all aspects will require your attention on a relatively equal basis. Failure to recognize this requirement occurs all too often. Why? Many new or inexperienced business owners, especially those who are entrepreneurial by nature, show a distinct tendency to concentrate their energies on whatever they are selling, at the expense of the other parts of the business. Or, they pour their energies into marketing and leave product/service and business operations to take care of themselves. For these people, routine business procedures are likely to come in a distant third.

Such tunnel vision can be serious enough to damage your business severely in the same way that a three-spoke wheel with two spokes missing will eventually cause an accident. While you focus on the product, the business runs itself into the ground, without proper attention to cash flow, taxes and other mundane matters. Or lack of attention to marketing results, eventually, in little or no new business. Fortunately, as you train yourself to recognize potential pitfalls, you can avoid, correct or compensate for them.

Don't Assume that Scheduling of Projects and People Is Routine

It may look easy enough to schedule people and projects, particularly if you follow the guidelines in Chapter 2, to *Establish Systems for Working with Employee and/or Independent Contractors* and *Manage Time Efficiently*. But don't believe it! There can be as many pitfalls as there are projects and people you depend on to get the work done.

You can avoid some of them by establishing a generous amount of lead time for projects, and lining up the people you need, well in advance. But in any undertaking where you have two or more people and/or companies involved, the opportunities for something to go wrong are infinite. At these times, corrective action strategies are crucial.

Manufacturers must have more than one source for raw materials, to allow for the inevitable day that a regular supplier can't provide an essential component, an alternate labor pool or reliable temporary help to compensate for an outbreak of illness and, when necessary, the willingness to admit to a customer that an order will be delayed. Retailers should have more than one supplier/distributor for products and a source for temporary help. Service firms, at first glance, may face fewer pitfalls with scheduling since they don't make or sell products. However, because they often require people with highly specialized skills, they may have to overcome more difficult obstacles if someone with a particular skill isn't available when needed. These backup sources are equally invaluable when there are scheduling conflicts.

Don't Underestimate the Influence of New Technology or Competition

Sometimes you can see a new development ahead of time and make the necessary changes to prevent your company from falling behind. But technological developments or a major competitor can appear so suddenly that you have no advance warning. What then? In these circumstances, swift corrective action procedures are essential. You must be in a position to swing into action with sufficient money to modify, add to or replace what you sell and, probably, develop new marketing/advertising strategies as well.

Compensating for this pitfall is likely to be hardest and most difficult for manufacturers who must develop a new product and/or purchase new, expensive equipment for making that product. Wholesale and retail sales firms can usually compensate rapidly and at much less expense by adding to, or replacing, items in their stock. Service firms can sometimes adapt their services quickly, or add new ones to meet new competition; occasionally, a technological advance will require these firms to locate independent contractors with the new skills or hire additional employees to maintain their market position.

Watch Out for Changing Conditions and Regulations

In today's complex world, new laws and government regulations governing such matters as safety, air quality control, disposal of hazardous wastes—the list is endless—can change your company's working conditions overnight, whether you manufacture or sell products affected by legislation and regulations, or provide a service that requires you to have current knowledge of these changes.

The recent Americans with Disabilities Act, as an example, makes many changes mandatory for manufacturers who now have to provide certain facilities for disabled employees, for retailers who must provide proper access for disabled customers, and for human resources training firms who must incorporate the new requirements into their training programs.

Having read about these common pitfalls, you now have—or can make—a list of the ones you've had to deal with in your own business. Although the ones in this chapter don't begin to cover all types of problems that crop up, they are the ones that were mentioned most often in my informal survey of small business owners. Their primary value lies in alerting you to their existence as well as strategies for handling them.

Your Turn   *Answer the following:*

- ▶ Identify at least two pitfalls you have had to face since you started your business.

- ▶ How did each affect your business?

- ▶ How did you overcome the problems?

- ▶ List three changes that have occurred in your area of business since you began your own business.

PREVENT TYPICAL PRATFALLS

I could have based this entire section on errors of judgment I have made over the years, pratfalls that occurred because I was in a hurry and took an unwarranted risk, or because I failed to listen to an inner voice that, for want of a better label, I call "common sense" or "gut feeling." I still cringe when I think of mistakes that should never have happened, and I suspect that you do, too. If so, you're not alone!

When I was gathering information on pratfalls from other small business owners—trading horror stories—I was surprised to find how many had made the same kinds of mistakes. This made me realize that, while business owners differ markedly from each other as people, they share many of the same flaws in judgment, at least in the initial stages of learning how to operate a business. I also realized how important this information can be, since correcting mistakes can run costs up to astronomical heights. When it comes to pratfalls, the proverbial "ounce of prevention" is truly worth a pound of cure!

As you read, take comfort in knowing that other business owners have made similar mistakes and, most important, you will be able to avoid making some of these mistakes in the future!

Spend Money Only on Genuine Needs

Be careful not to spend money foolishly. This should be item one in every small business owner's list of "no-nos." Nothing is more exhilarating than to buy glossy new furniture or equipment to create an office or plant appearance you don't need. Nothing is more depressing than to see the bills come in for these purchases, when you are short on money for materials, equipment or services to maintain or develop your business. The range of foolish purchases is probably limitless; here are some typical examples that have created financial problems for small business owners I interviewed:

► "Expensive offices with space we didn't use until we'd been in business five years."

► "Equipment leased in order to get fancier models; the lease costs would have paid for the same equipment in a year."

► "Expensive furniture for a reception area that clients seldom if ever saw."

► "A mobile phone I didn't need and couldn't afford to use."

► "Fancy brochures in three colors that cost an arm and a leg, and never did anything for our image or anything else."

► "The top of the line overhead projector for workshops that was so powerful we had trouble focusing it in the training rooms we usually had to work in."

► "A binding machine plus binding materials that we almost never use; it was such a good deal I couldn't pass it up."

- ▶ "A lifetime supply of cheap stick pens that we'll never use; after five years in storage, many of them refuse to work."

- ▶ "After our first large contract, we spent thousands of dollars on public relations; what we got was public relations, but not any more business."

- ▶ "Advertising that cost a lot but didn't reach our market; I should have known better."

- ▶ "A whole new line of canned foods at a wonderful bargain that none of our customers would buy."

- ▶ "An automated machine tool system with ten functions; we have never needed more than five of the functions."

The next time you see a wonderful widget for sale with lots of bells and whistles, plus flashing neon lights, remember this list. Don't spend your hard earned money on it.

Don't Become Too Dependent on One Large Customer or Client

While this pratfall doesn't apply to retail sales firms, it often applies to small manufacturing and service companies. This can be a very large and serious mistake, because nothing looks better to a small company than a large account. Unfortunately, it's all too easy to become so accustomed to receiving large orders and renewed contracts from these customers that you virtually ignore the necessity to keep looking for other new business.

A firm that manufactures precision parts depended on one large aerospace company for most of its business. When that account evaporated after several years, the manufacturer was left with very little business, a large number of employees and a sizable overhead. In another case, almost the same thing occurred. A maintenance service for computers had a contract with a large insurance company that renewed the contract annually for six years and accounted for over 75 percent of the firm's gross income. When the client downsized its operations, the small business was left virtually without business for several months. On the plus side, those were months when the two owners really began to learn how to run a small business. Both firms have recovered nicely at this point, but it was an expensive lesson.

Follow Quality Control Measures Strictly

I was really surprised at how often this pratfall occurs. Apparently, after a period of success a false sense of security develops. The small business owner is lulled into an attitude of complacency, or has so much business that under the pressure of time, he simply doesn't follow carefully his own quality control procedures.

You don't require many examples to see how this can damage your business. A manufacturing firm working on a rush order didn't calibrate its measuring gauges for the parts it had made; the entire order had to be done over. A retail cleaners stopped making weekly checks of the large, revolving mechanized unit that held clothes ready for customers, because nothing had ever been wrong with it; one day, a belt broke and hundreds of cleaned, pressed clothes had to be cleaned and pressed again. A consulting firm failed to proofread some publicity material for their new book; it came out with a couple of glaring errors, in two colors. The answer, of course, is to resist any urge to take shortcuts in quality control.

Only Accept New Business You're Sure You Can Handle

Small businesses are particularly prone to this pratfall, because they suffer most from the feast or famine syndrome—too much or not enough business. It's tempting for them to take on work, no matter how busy they are. The problem arises when it becomes extremely difficult, if not impossible, for manufacturers and service firms to meet their commitments on time, and they lose accounts because of it.

Another form of this problem is taking on work without the facilities or skills to handle it. In manufacturing, the problem may be lack of the proper equipment to produce what's required. In retail sales, it may be lack of space to store or display certain merchandise. In service firms, the work may not be within the range of the owner's skills or field of expertise. All of these mean that you are in over your head in one way or another, cannot provide proper customer service, and inevitably lose business or damage your reputation.

Take in a Partner Only After Thorough Advance Investigation

For a small business owner, often working on a limited budget and sometimes in isolation from outside stimulation, taking in a partner can be a wise move. More capital, more help and another person to share ideas and responsibilities, are all ideal for developing and expanding a small business—provided the new partner is the right one. The wrong partner, one whose personal traits and business skills do not complement and augment the skills of the other, can, in a worst case scenario, saddle the original owner with a shark intent on devouring profits, clients and/or the entire business. At best, such a partnership is certain to end in what often turns out to be an unpleasant business "divorce."

Horror stories abound. One owner who had spent enormous amounts of time and energy developing a profitable consulting business, took in a partner who had little money but a great deal of expertise with computers, excellent computer equipment and many ideas for further expanding the business. In a few months, the new partner had used his expertise and computer equipment to steal the company's client records and to manipulate the poorly designed partnership agreement in such a way that the original owner nearly lost control of the business. The damage was extensive, but with some expensive legal help, the owner prevented the takeover and installed safeguards to protect the company in the future.

The key to avoiding this pratfall is advance preparation, to make sure that the partners can and will work well together. Great advice, but how do you choose the right person? In an article in the January 8, 1990 issue of *Working World* Magazine,

Lee Gardenswartz, Ph.D. and Anita Rowe, Ph.D., partners for twelve years in the management consulting firm of Gardenswartz & Rowe, identified criteria and characteristics that mark a successful partnership:

1. *Shared Values:* It is essential for partners to have the same beliefs about "honesty, excellence and morality." Without this, the partnership cannot succeed.

2. *Equivalent Contributions:* Partners need to contribute equivalent time, money and energy to the business; otherwise, resentment develops over who does what and how much of what is fair.

3. *Interpersonal Skills:* While they certainly don't need to be Siamese twins, both partners must possess certain people skills "such as a sense of humor, ability to communicate and open-mindedness."

4. *Well-Balanced Approaches and Personal Styles:* Here, instead of sharing the same traits, the partners need to complement and balance each other; one may be good at analysis and the other at synthesis; one may like to concentrate on details, while the other focuses on the large picture; one may have special sales ability and the other is full of creative ideas. And so on.

To forge a successful partnership, the two people must sit down together and explore their mutual values, contributions, individual skills and personal styles. Out of this session, they can assess their potential as partners and, where necessary, devise ways to compensate for anything they lack, or work out plans to develop what they need.

Your Turn

Answer the following:

► Into what pratfalls has your business fallen?

► How much money have you lost on pratfalls?

► Have you ever taken in a partner?

► If so, what factors did you consider?

► Would you consider anything else now?

PREPARE FOR MAJOR DISASTERS

You may never have to experience a major disaster. Most business owners don't. But natural disasters such as fires, social ones such as recessions, and personal ones such as serious illness happen often enough to put preparations against them high on your list of priorities. The bumper sticker "One nuclear bomb can ruin your whole day" is a masterpiece of understatement. The same idea applies to business. One earthquake, a riot or a major illness can put you out of business overnight.

But what can you do other than carry the proper insurance? Surprisingly enough, there are quite a few ways to protect yourself; some are simple and inexpensive, others are more elaborate and costly. The important thing is to consider ways in which you and your business are vulnerable and take whatever steps are necessary to protect yourself.

Establish Safeguards Against Natural Disasters

As a California resident, I may be more aware than business owners in other states of the dangers of earthquakes, fires, floods and other major upheavals of nature. But, if you find yourself, as I did, sitting alone in a pitch black office with no power after an earthquake, you will be glad to have flashlights and/or candles handy. I waited a moment to see if anything else was going to happen, and then reached behind my work station to the lateral file cabinet that holds client records. In the bottom drawer was the large flashlight I'd put there a year before. That beam of light was a welcome sight. With it, I found my way to the front office door and looked out into the hallway where skylights illuminated what seemed to be an intact building. The only damage was a few books that had dive-bombed off bookshelves and a couple of pieces of equipment jarred out of place.

A few years ago, another company wasn't so lucky. The area had been having exceptionally heavy rains; the owner arrived at the office one morning to find it two inches deep in water from a horrendous waterfall coming through a broken piece of ceiling tile. They lost supplies and furniture. They had to move into another office in the same building for months, while the building owners first tried to locate and repair the leak(s), and then replaced the entire roof. In the meantime, the company's soggy quarters were stripped, recarpeted and repainted.

To some extent, insurance helped both firms. But nothing could replace the lost records, although the owner fortunately didn't lose all records and equipment. Had the downpour through the roof occurred in the inner office, the devastation would have been enormous.

In another recent instance, a neighborhood restaurant, owned by a husband and wife, was wiped out by a fire that started from defective wiring and engulfed the entire premises. While they had insurance, it was far less than they needed; they could not start over.

Insurance, probably double what many businesses carry now, is a prime step in preparing for a natural disaster. Other steps are to provide emergency equipment, food and, for companies who have irreplaceable records, a fireproof safe. All of these measures cost money, but nothing like the amount it could cost to stay in business should a disaster occur.

Protect Yourself from Social Disasters

There may be a few recession-proof small businesses; most have been, are or will be severely affected by the recession that the United States has suffered from recently, to say nothing of the damage caused in California and New York by community riots. Recessions, riots, wars—these social disasters have a negative influence on businesses of all sizes, particularly on the small businesses that serve or supply larger companies and local communities.

What can you do to protect yourself in these circumstances? Sometimes, not much. A recession that goes on too long or a riot that destroys a neighborhood can severely damage the healthiest small business. Again, insurance can offer more protection than you might expect; a reserve fund to handle six months' operating expenses can provide an invaluable cushion for loss of income and rebuilding.

Three small manufacturing companies located in the same industrial complex sustained major damage when a block of buildings burned to the ground. Of the two companies that carried minimum insurance against catastrophes, one went out of business; the other one had a cash reserve large enough to enable them to resume business within four months. The third company had enough insurance and cash reserves to rebuild and start up operation again in sixty days.

A wholesaler and a television store both lost their entire stock during riots in Los Angeles. The wholesaler was unable to recover from the loss. Knowing his stock was always vulnerable to theft, the television store owner carried heavy insurance; he was back in business in ten days.

A flash flood in an Arizona community inundated the business area, flooding several blocks of businesses. The two owners of a word processing service lost their computers and work in progress, but salvaged their client and other business records, which were kept on disks in a fireproof file on top of a worktable.

The common thread running through all these examples is that foresight, while it cannot prevent social disasters, can do much to protect you from sometimes catastrophic effects or, at least, help you recover from them.

Establish Emergency Procedures in Case of Personal Injury or Illness

The circumstances in this type of disaster differ radically from the other two types. A small business running along smoothly is suddenly disrupted when the owner suffers an accident or illness. If there is a partner or other management person familiar with the business, that person can usually take over for a time and continue the business with little or no interruption. But what about the one-person firm or a company with one owner, and a clerk or other employee without special skills or management experience? In a few instances, the business can go on hold until the owner recovers. In many instances, however, work in progress, new work commitments and office operations must continue if the business is to survive.

Assuming that the interruption will be a matter of weeks or months at most, there are several possible alternate courses of action. One is to put a family member or trusted friend temporarily in charge, to handle phone calls, pay bills and, where appropriate, make arrangements with clients and suppliers to delay completing work in progress. Another, if the firm has made consistent use of outside services and perhaps independent contractors to perform parts of the work, is to delegate the work on hand to one or more of these companies and people. A third alternative is to hire someone on a temporary basis to operate the company.

I had plenty of time to think about this type of disaster a few years ago. After what I thought was a minor physical problem, I went for some medical tests. One week later, I was in the hospital contemplating a huge bandage over the surgical site, and watching the IV bubble into my veins. I was out of commission for approximately a month; during that time, I used the first alternative described above; a close friend who had done some work for my company took over and handled everything magnificently, on no notice.

What can *you* do to prepare for the possibility of something happening to you? First, put essential routines and procedures *in writing*. I was lucky to have a friend who knew how my company operated. Then, look around among your family and friends to see who could stand in for you temporarily, on short notice; give that person a short, crash course on what he or she would have to do in case of need. Failing that, or in addition to it, contact your outside providers and/or contractors and give them a crash course in how to proceed if you're not around.

If the nature of your work is such that none of these alternatives would be possible, then *write down* your instructions for putting the company on hold while you are incapacitated.

Awareness that this kind of personal disaster can occur even if you consider yourself in top health (I did) means you are halfway to a workable answer. Advance instructions and preparation is the other half of the solution. But don't stay up nights worrying. Once you've established whatever emergency procedures you can, continue your regular routine. The majority of owners operate their businesses for many years without having to deal with any of the disasters detailed in this chapter.

Your Turn

Answer the following:

▶ Could you continue in business if your records were destroyed?

▶ Could you continue in business if your equipment was destroyed?

▶ Do you have insurance to replace your equipment, if necessary?

▶ Could your company continue to operate if you were unable to run it for an extended period?

▶ Do you have emergency procedures, in case of personal injury or illness?

ASK YOURSELF

▶ Discuss the following statement that most closely describes your policy in handling possible pitfalls:

a. I make sure I don't neglect any aspect of my business in favor of others.

b. I keep close watch on new technology and/or competition.

c. I keep informed about changing business conditions and/or regulations that affect my company.

▶ Considering your personality and temperament, comment on the following types of pratfalls that are most likely to occur:

a. Spending money on things I don't need

b. Becoming dependent on one or two large clients

c. Neglecting consistent quality controls in order to get the work out on time

d. Taking on business I can't handle

▶ Compare the specific advantages and disadvantages of taking in a partner at some point in expanding your business.

▶ Considering your type of business, your age and the location of your company, which of the following types of natural disasters are most likely to require careful preparation?

a. Earthquake, fire, hurricanes, etc.

b. Personal illness or injury

c. Recession or seasonal variations in business demand

d. A rapidly changing field and/or market

Describe that preparation.

CHAPTER FOUR

DEVELOPING MARKETING AND ADVERTISING SYSTEMS

PLAN AHEAD!

Guiding Principle: Plan Ahead! The three best times to do marketing and advertising are when business is poor, when it is satisfactory and when it is great—in other words, continuously!

This guiding principle may appear extreme. It's not. It applies consistently to any successful business. While several elements operate together to make your business profitable, the omission of well planned marketing strategies is a guarantee of failure. To develop systems that work best for you, keep in mind the relationship between marketing and advertising. Marketing efforts, broadly speaking, are directed towards identifying your customer/client base and increasing the number of potential buyers of your product or service—in other words, expanding your market. Advertising, which is a part of marketing, consists of the media and techniques you use to persuade potential buyers to become actual ones.

A large majority of small business owners recognize that some form of marketing or advertising is essential. The problem lies in knowing how to approach it, how much to do, how often to do it, and how much time and money to spend. Those who don't plan ahead are certain to run into trouble. Lulled into a false sense of security by several months or a year or two of steady increases in gross profit, they find it easy to devote little thought or money to the question of how to increase business. For these owners, the results are predictable. At some point, they will find themselves facing a future containing little or no new business. This is the time when many new businesses either collapse or come perilously close to going under. Those who make it past this point, usually by working lots of "eight-day" weeks, and sometimes only after an infusion of new capital, have learned exactly how crucial it is to make continuous efforts to replace former customers and add new ones. Fortunately, while these late bloomers are scrambling to stay afloat, they also develop marketing techniques that are effective without requiring huge sums of money.

Another marketing problem among small business owners is the one I call the "too little, too late" syndrome. Few small businesses can afford large marketing and advertising budgets, but spending only a little money now and then is as deadly to success as total lack of foresight. It just takes a little longer to kill the business.

After years of working for others, two experienced beauty operators decided to buy their own salon. When they found a shop, they put a lot of money and sweat equity into new, bright paint and equipment. Shortly after that, an operator left and they didn't replace her. At that point, they had three operators: themselves and one other. They also had two unoccupied work stations. Slowly, over the next few years, long-time clients died or moved away. Since the owners were doing nothing to replace them, business went down. Eventually, they sent out mailers to reach new people in the neighborhood, but one day when someone contacted them about trying other local advertising, one owner said, "Not if it costs me anything." Within another six months, business was so poor that they decided not to renew the lease on their shop.

If you apply the step-by-step marketing procedures and choose wisely among the options discussed in this chapter, you will be able to take advantage of what others have had to learn the hard way—and at the same time avoid either the "no marketing" or the "too little, too late" marketing errors:

► Identify Your Target Groups

► Develop a Marketing/Advertising Plan, Schedule and Budget

► Track Your Results and Modify Your Marketing Plan

IDENTIFY YOUR TARGET GROUPS

You must gain an initial idea of who your potential buyers are before you plunge into marketing plans and strategies, and invest time, money and effort that may or may not be well spent. One approach is to buy one or more of the marketing books available by the dozen in any bookstore. Invariably, these books tell you to conduct "marketing research," to identify the people and/or companies who have a need or desire for what you offer. It's a great idea, in theory. If you have the staff available to set up research studies and the budget to support them, by all means do so.

You don't have that kind of staff or money? Neither do the majority of small business owners. But that doesn't mean that your marketing effort is doomed from the start. Nor does it mean that you have to hire an outside expert to conduct the research for you. In fact, help is probably no farther away than you own business records. Examine your materials invoices, billing and delivery documents, purchase records and sales receipts—anything that contains information about who has purchased what products or services from you, in what quantities and with what frequency. These records will yield an amazing amount of data about the companies and people who have already done business with you—data you can use to develop an accurate profile of potential buyers.

Step One: Examine Your Customer List or Sales Receipts

This is an excellent starting point. If you have been in business for a year or more, you can identify potential new business by analyzing the people and/or companies who already have bought what you sell.

Examine your Accounts Receivable and paid Customer Receipts for the last six months or preferably a year. Make a list that includes as much of the following information as possible. For your present purpose, close estimates will be nearly as useful as facts:

- ▶ *Company size:* small (up to 100 employees); medium (100 to 300 or 400); or large (over 400)

- ▶ *Location:* area of city, county, state or territory the customer facilities or office is in

- ▶ *Kinds of product(s) purchased:* one type only, two or three products, or the entire range of what you produce

- ▶ *Quantity and frequency of purchases:* small orders now and then, moderate orders frequently, large orders at specified intervals, etc.

- ▶ *Financial status:* pay on time, a little slow, or quite slow, etc.

▶ *Characteristics of their customers (the ones they sell your products to):* age, range, special interest groups, poor or wealthy, companies or individuals, men or women, etc.

▶ *Other:* The above list covers many general characteristics of customers. If your products are specialized (baby toys, medical garments, cosmetics, etc.), you might identify another range of characteristics for your customers or the customers of the companies who buy your products.

Your sales receipts and purchasing records will tell you a good deal about what products in your store sell best and how expensive they are. Close examination will allow you to speculate on some matters: the financial status of the majority of people who buy from you, their special preferences and interests, their age range, sex, etc. If you own a local retail grocery store, you can also make an informal assessment of who your customers are by direct observation. This method takes time and concentration, but a few days spent observing customers and making a few notes on age range, sex, apparent financial status and product preferences will help you identify the best prospects for new business.

Had the beauty shop owners conducted this type of examination, they would have realized that many of their clients who had been with them for a long time were also in or approaching their senior years of life—a fact that could have alerted the owners, much earlier, to the inevitable loss of clients as time went on.

Some service firms sell to companies; others sell their services to individuals; some do both. If your clients are companies, your analysis will include most or all of the kinds of data described below for manufacturers and wholesalers, with particular attention to the kind of business each client operates (insurance, computer software, banking, etc.), the type(s) of service you provide for each type of business, how much business each type of client does with you and, of course, the size of each company. If you provide management training and your best clients are large insurance firms and banks, you have already identified some essential characteristics of your potential new business.

If your service business is aimed at individuals, your analysis will focus on the people who use your services. One woman who runs her word processing service out of her home provides reports, term papers, letters, resumés and, sometimes, proposals. These two examples illustrate an important point. You can't rely on someone else's statistics to identify major characteristics of your customers.

When you have completed the examination of your clients, you will also have completed step one of a marketing research study that has certainly cost something in time and energy, but nothing in consultant or other research fees.

Step Two: Select the Best Customers from Your List

Step two in identifying a target group for your marketing efforts uses the information you collected about your customers. Go through the list and select your best customers or types of customers. Make another list, again listing their principal characteristics: company size, location, types of product or service they buy from you, financial status and, for individual clients or customers, their age range, sex, etc. But *don't* throw away the larger, first list with its data on many of your clients; you will use that list later for what I think of as secondary target groups for marketing. If this seems to be an unnecessary repetition of work, I assure you it isn't.

When I took myself through this process, I discovered that my best clients were neither the smallest nor the largest companies, but those in between the two extremes, companies with 100 to 500 employees. Once I had this information, it seemed self-evident that smaller firms either didn't need or couldn't afford to buy the manuals we produce; larger ones had their own in-house departments or technical writers who wrote whatever they needed. It was the middle-sized group that needed and could afford our services. Let me emphasize, however, that this "self-evident" information wasn't evident at all until I examined the information I collected about my clients over a period of two or three years.

At this point, a picture of the companies and people who buy what you offer should begin to emerge. This is your target group for establishing your first marketing and advertising strategies.

A local manufacturer of machine tools who hired a marketing consultant to perform this process found, as I had, that his best customers were middle-sized producers of small machine parts.

Another manufacturing company who produced automated tooling systems had thought their best customers were the very large firms with high volume. To their surprise, they discovered that they were getting almost as much business from a number of quite small firms who bought one or two smaller systems to reduce labor costs.

A retail drug store who had been stocking many kinds of cosmetics and perfumes favored by the young found that the majority of its customers were married, middle-aged and older women who purchased quite different products.

A printing company discovered a previously unrecognized group of potential customers for letterheads and envelopes—those who initially bought inexpensive stationery, but who later ordered more elaborate designs and logos.

Your analysis of your best customers may not result in dramatic discoveries, but you will certainly have a clear, focused conglomerate "portrait" of those who, together, provide the bulk of your business.

Secondary Sources: Use Your Refined List to Locate New Markets and Customers

Up to this point, you will use what researchers refer to as "primary sources"—in this case, data collected about your past and present buyers. Now is the time to turn to secondary sources to identify and locate similar potential prospects around which you will build your marketing/advertising plan and schedule. These sources take widely different forms; the major ones are people, magazines, newspapers, books, commercial lists and reports. Although some books and materials are in a library, I strongly recommend that you buy at least a few so that you can check or highlight items and make marginal notes as needed.

Networking to develop contacts with people who might become customers normally requires time and money for membership fees in organizations. Participation in trade shows, local community volunteer groups, chambers of commerce and similar groups will also require time and money. But, with the exception of trade shows, none of these demands a large budget or ongoing financial outlay. Magazines and newspapers, appropriate to what you sell, involve relatively small costs, and can be invaluable sources.

Commercial lists geared to the people and businesses you would like to reach can cost anything from modest to fairly large sums of money. There are also specialized directories or buyers guides that list thousands of business firms. Available throughout the western states is a series of fifteen directories, published by the Database Publishing Company in Newport Beach, California, that contain much valuable marketing information about many companies: address, major officers, type of business, number of employees, etc. My company uses the Southern California Directory and Buyers Guide as a major secondary source for locating potential new clients. This particular book, revised annually, costs between $100 and $200—not a large investment for a book so valuable to manufacturers and service firms in particular. In other parts to the country, similar books are surely available.

Use the publications or lists you have acquired in two ways: go through the entries to identify additional companies—individuals if you're using a specialized list—that are similar to your own list of best customers and located within your current selling area or territory. Also look for those in nearby geographical areas or regions, to which you can reasonably extend your company's business. If your local area has enough potential buyers of your products or services, begin your search in that area. When you have exhausted the potential within that region, expand the search to include additional communities adjacent to your local area. While the nature of your business, its location and your limits for territory expansion will be the major determinants of the sources you choose, certain sources are especially valuable for particular types of business.

A buyers guide or directory of manufacturing firms for your region is of great value. The *1992 California Manufacturers Register* (published by Database Publishing Co.) for example, gives information about more than 24,000 manufacturing companies in California. Trade journals for each type of business are also resources for manufacturing. I once worked for a trade journal based in Chicago, Illinois, which contained articles, ads and news stories directed exclusively at the commercial baking industry. I confess that in the course of my work there, I learned more about baking ovens and other equipment than I ever wanted to know, but a manufacturing firm whose products are used in that industry would find that trade journal a gold mine for potential new business. Many trade associations also have their own publications.

For wholesalers, there are trade publications for different products; articles and ads alike yield information of value to a wholesale company seeking to expand its business. There are fewer publications and guides for those who operate small retail stores; for these owners, there are catalogs of merchandise that appear in the mail, without charge and often in great abundance. Examining these and other materials related to whatever you sell may open up possibilities for new lines of merchandise that can bring new and additional customers to your store.

In service fields, secondary sources vary widely from one type of service to another. Associations, usually with at least one publication and often with a membership directory, exist for everything from personnel agencies and consultants in many fields, through health care and realtors, to trainers and travel agencies. You name it, there's probably an association for it! If you aren't already aware of at least one association and/or publication related to your field, a trip to the local library's reference section should help you locate one or more.

Whatever source or sources you use to identify companies and/or individuals similar to your present customers, when you have completed this task you should have enough new leads to launch your actual marketing efforts.

Your Turn

Answer the following:

► List your present buyers.

► List your top selling product or service.

► From which buyers do you receive the most repeat business?

Worksheet: Identifying Target Group Characteristics

A. Major Characteristics of Present and Past Customers and Clients

Individuals
1. Age Range: children, teenagers, young adults, adults, seniors
2. Sex: mostly male, mostly female, both
3. Financial Levels: below average, average, above average

Companies
1. Number of employees: up to 50, 50 to 100, 100 to 500, more
2. Location: neighborhood, community, city, state, other
3. Kinds of products/services purchased
4. Frequency and volume of purchases
5. Financial status: pay on time, a little slow, quite slow

B. Major Characteristics of Best Customers and Clients

Individuals
1. Age range: _____
2. Sex: _____
3. Financial levels: _____

Companies
1. Number of employees: _____
2. Location: _____
3. Kinds of products/services purchased: _____
4. Frequency and volume of purchases: _____
5. Financial status: _____

C. Major Characteristics of Second Best Customers and Clients

Individuals
List the same kind of information identified above.

Companies
List the same kind of information identified above.

DEVELOP A MARKETING AND ADVERTISING PLAN, SCHEDULE AND BUDGET

Once you have a set of leads produced according to the steps detailed in this chapter, you are prepared to develop a marketing effort focused on companies and/or individuals who are most likely to become new customers. As you pursue your marketing efforts, you will discover that the time and energy invested in identifying your target group has been well spent. It will take anywhere from a third to fifty percent less time to achieve good results than would be necessary if you simply shot a few marketing or advertising arrows into the air and hoped for the best.

Basic to a successful program is your personal commitment to marketing. Without commitment, your efforts may be sporadic, random and predictably less than completely successful. When you have realized that marketing is essential, you then need to consider it as a regular part of the cost of doing business, as necessary as paying rent. One way to achieve this perspective is to think of marketing, not as an extra cost, but as a current business investment that will pay off later in increased profits. Finally, look at marketing as much more than one or more "things" you do to increase business. Good marketing involves building an integrated, interrelated, well coordinated program whose elements work together in your own marketing plan and schedule.

Establish a Budget

This is part of your commitment—establish a budget, however small at first, that goes only for marketing and advertising. I am not talking big bucks. One company's first budget consisted of about $300, devoted to producing a sales letter and mailing it directly to several hundred potential customers. Since the owner didn't yet have a plan or a strategy, didn't know that she could expect only 1 to $1\frac{1}{2}$ percent response from a direct mailing, and didn't know that selling by mail comes in a distant third to contacts in person and by phone, that effort failed. The mailing wasn't a total loss, however; the owner learned from it, and received a bonus a year later, in the form of a phone call from a company manager who had kept her letter. The call resulted in several small jobs over the next several years.

The size of your budget will depend on the group you want to reach, how you intend to reach that group, and at what intervals you plan to follow up on your initial contact. This means that the initial budget will be tentative until you are further along in your plans. However, a real budget will help you establish some limits for your efforts, and bypass plans calling for expensive materials, layouts and media beyond your financial reach.

Examine Various Media and Approaches

This is an enormous topic, worthy of a book in its own right. There are hundreds of books about how to market your product or services. Some, like *Marketing Your Consulting or Professional Services* by David Karlson, Ph.D. (published by Crisp Publications), are directed to specific types of businesses. If you find one geared to your field of business that is both practical and concise, by all means get it. Just avoid a tome weighing over two pounds—you'll never read it. I read a great many articles and short books in the course of my self-directed crash course in marketing for my company and learned something from each publication.

There are also some basics you can master in a relatively short time. Selecting the media that will probably work best is a good starting point. There are only three kinds of media: print, audio and audiovisual. Print media include advertising directories (*Yellow Pages*), flyers, direct or bulk mailing, newspapers, magazines and signs or banners. Unless you have an extra half million or so to spend, you can eliminate large newspaper and magazine ads and concentrate on one or more of the others as possibilities.

Audio (sound) media, practical for advertising, consist of radio and telemarketing. Radio commercials can reach a large audience in a local or national area. For most small businesses, national radio commercials are too expensive and probably would overshoot your target group—like using a shotgun to kill a flea. Local radio, however, can be very effective, especially for retailers and some service industries. That's a choice that might be appropriate for your firm, although it won't be the cheapest advertising around. Telemarketing, currently on the rise as a marketing/advertising/selling medium, is often considered to be a high pressure, intrusive approach that you might reject without a second thought. Used ethically and professionally, however, telemarketing can be a cost effective way for a surprising number and range of small businesses, from manufacturing to service companies, to reach specific potential clients.

Audiovisual media, other than personal presentations before live audiences, are of four kinds: television, videotapes, sales representatives and networking. You can probably exclude television and most videotaped presentations as much too expensive—at first anyway. Of the other two audiovisual media, networking to make contacts at organizational meetings is by far the least costly and, for some companies, very effective. Sales people, whether on base-plus-commission or straight commission, are essential for some types of marketing and are indispensable in certain industries and service fields for selling. However, since sales people are employees, their use commits you to all the legal and tax requirements involved in having employees; you need to include this fact in your thinking as you develop your marketing plan.

Even from this brief discussion of the various media available, you can see that choosing one or more media can be complex. To simplify the selection, make your choices according to these basic criteria:

▶ *Cost:* Eliminate it from your available options if it costs more than your budget will allow. Even within your budget, avoid shooting everything you have on one approach or on a one time effort. Think in terms of a plan to be executed over a period of time, suitable for your company, target group, number of new leads and amount of new business you can handle.

▶ *Suitability for your product or service:* Banners and bulk mailings, effective for retail sales and service businesses like pizza places, maintenance and gardening, are not normally suitable for manufacturing and professional services companies.

▶ *Suitability for your target group:* Keep in mind the size and location of the group you're trying to reach. It's a waste of money to choose media that are too limited or reach beyond your group and area.

Your preliminary examination of available media based on the above criteria will reduce your options considerably and will simplify your final choice or choices for the next step in developing your marketing plan.

Select the Proper Media and Approach

While some marketing approaches and media are effective in more than one type of business, keep in mind that what works well for one type of firm may be totally ineffective for another. Only you can make the final decisions for your marketing effort, but there are some guidelines to help.

For manufacturers, brochures and flyers that describe your product line, its capabilities and its specifications can be very effective if mailed to the proper person(s) at companies who use the products you make. A machine tool company sends a preliminary flyer listing products and their uses in response to initial inquiries, as well as to companies that could use these tools. If these contacts show further interest by returning a tear-off on the flyer, the company sends them a four-page color brochure with more detail about each product. This same company and a number of others in similar industrial fields also place small, carefully written ads in technical publications geared to their specific industry and area. Another company that uses a similar approach, also has a videotape of one of its products in commercial use that it sends to companies who have expressed more than a superficial interest in buying. In addition, most manufacturers have sales representatives to make initial and follow-up contacts.

Wholesalers of certain products, such as cosmetics, use media and approaches similar to those used by manufacturers, although wholesale items are likely to rely even more heavily on sales representatives to introduce and sell their products. Retail sales firms use a wide variety of print media for their marketing and advertising. All of the relatively inexpensive approaches—banners for "Grand Openings" and sales, flyers for bulk mailings, and neighborhood distribution, coupon books issued by local companies, neighborhood sales booklets, and direct mailings aimed at specific target groups—can be effective if the company sends them out in sufficient quantity, at frequent enough intervals to make an impact on potential buyers.

Here, there is a wide division between types of services. Trade services such as gardening, electrical work, painting, roof repairing, etc., that contact individual customers directly, use newspapers, *Yellow Pages* display ads, flyers, bulk and direct mailings and, occasionally, local radio spots to reach their target groups. Many of the very small individual or family-owned concerns go door-to-door, leaving cards and flyers.

In contrast, professional services such as consultants, computer and word processing experts, trainers, etc.—although they may send brochures to selected companies and place ads in special sections of local newspapers designed for graphics design, financial, legal, accounting and other similar services—rely more on other approaches. The traditional one is networking for contacts and referrals at chamber of commerce, volunteer and professional organization meetings. Once known as a "good old boys" network, it is now used extensively by men and women alike. And, increasingly, many service companies are making greater use of telemarketing which, properly designed and controlled, can be highly effective.

I certainly count myself as an enthusiastic convert to professional telemarketing. After a number of mostly ineffective attempts to contact my target groups through a series of direct mailings and limited networking, I decided to try telemarketing—not to sell my services, but to *introduce* them to key management people in target companies. Because I wrote my own scripts, I set the tone as professional, low-key and informal. Bingo! Once I had located a good telemarketer, my set of 4 × 6 inch lead cards, painstakingly compiled from the

Southern California Buyers Guide, began to turn into new business at a brisk rate, especially when I followed up each productive telephone introduction by mailing—first class only—a packet containing a cover sales letter and sample pages from procedures we had written. Telemarketing is not only cost effective on a part-time basis, it has been my single best marketing approach for several years.

As a not so incidental note, I read somewhere that actors make excellent telemarketers. It's true. They have nerves of steel that do not collapse under the inevitable refusals; they are persistent enough to keep calling until they reach a key contact person at each company; they can adopt any tone you want them to and they are usually happy to have part-time work.

Establish a Marketing Schedule

Once you have selected the target group and media most appropriate for your company, your next step is to establish a schedule that specifies how often you use each type of media and approach. Only with a schedule can you properly monitor your marketing efforts and determine what works best, what is cost effective and what needs to be modified or eliminated. Although setting up a schedule may sound formidable, it is seldom as difficult as it seems. First, your efforts will necessarily be limited by the money available. Further, even if you have a considerable sum at your disposal, it is a good idea to begin small and expand, instead of attempting to mount a large, comprehensive marketing campaign. The obvious question at this point, of course, is how much of what to use, and at what intervals to use it. The answers lie partly in your choice of media, partly in the target group you want most to reach, and partly in the nature of your business.

There are a few general principles for establishing the frequency of your marketing efforts; these will be limited in their applicability to your business. The records you keep will be a more reliable guide, although there are always exceptions. You want to remain flexible in applying even your own track record. One general principle for advertising and marketing contacts is that potential buyers of your product or service will remember who you are only after you contact them a minimum of three times. Experience suggests that three contacts is a bit short of the typical number required to gain name recognition; sometimes it takes many more to reach highly desirable customers.

Another general principle is to follow up initial contacts relatively quickly, usually within a week or two, and then at fairly regular intervals of anywhere from once a month to once every two to six months, depending on the response you receive, current market conditions and the desirability of the potential buyer.

A third principle, seemingly contradictory to the second one, is not to make your contacts, especially those in person or by phone, so frequent that you irritate the person(s) you are trying to reach. In certain types of advertising, repetition to the point of nausea is a standard approach. Judging by the number of times some television and radio commercials are aired, this insane repetition must burn new pathways into the public's brains. However, for the purposes of a reasonable marketing schedule to be maintained within a specified budget, I do not recommend that approach.

A fourth principle is the one you will formulate for your own business, based on trial and error at the beginning and then, as you gain experience and confidence, on the results you achieve. This principle or set of principles will ultimately become the foundation for future marketing plans and schedules for your company. The examples that follow may assist you in setting up an initial marketing schedule:

Manufacturing:

- ▶ *Trade Journals:* For many manufacturers, well designed small display ads, in color if you can afford it, placed monthly or in every issue over a year's time are effective in tapping a large market.

- ▶ *Telemarketing:* Phone contacts, based on leads from a manufacturer's directory or buyer's guide for your area, over a period of weeks or months, can generate appointments or requests for brochures that lead to new business.

► *Sales Representatives:* Often there is no substitute for live contacts, preferably by appointments made in advance; these contacts must then be followed up promptly by phone calls, literature and/or letters, sent often enough to keep your company name and product line in the potential buyer's mind.

Retail Sales: Frequency of contact will vary enormously for retailers. To gain new business, a new hardware store, opened where none has been before, may only need to display a few banners announcing the opening and follow them up with bulk mailings once a month for three or four months. A fast-food outlet in an area with other fast-food outlets may need to send flyers every week, on a fairly continuous basis, to compete for the attention of potential buyers. It may also find it necessary to make special discount or coupon offers every two or three months to keep the firm's name and products before the public eye.

Services: Again, frequency will vary considerably, depending on the nature of the service. A word processing firm may have to contact potential users with great frequency at first and then, after establishing a reputation, get new business largely by referrals. Accountants may establish a similar marketing schedule, using some of the same media:

► *Newspapers:* Small 2 × 3 inch display ads, in special sections of newspapers that cover your selling area, reach your prospective buyers and fall within your budget, can work very well with three insertions at weekly intervals. After a lapse of two or three weeks, these can be followed up by another three insertions, and so on for at least four to six months. The effectiveness will depend on your service.

When a small office maintenance service tried this approach and schedule, the company received a deluge of job applications from workers displaced from local downsized industries. The owner had assumed that companies, as well as individuals, would refer to the section of the newspaper where he had placed his ad—apparently, they didn't. No building management companies ever responded to these ads.

▶ *Telemarketing:* As I said earlier in this chapter, scheduled properly, telemarketing can be extremely effective for service companies. I've had new clients greet us with joy at our first phone call; others have required many calls before achieving success. A random survey of a few companies who have become our clients within this last year yielded this information: company A required 6 calls over a six month period; company B required 5 calls over seven months; company C required more than 15 calls over fourteen months; and company D, a very large and desirable firm, didn't become our client until after 20 or so calls over a two-year period.

Your Turn

Answer the following:

▶ What is your present marketing/advertising cost per week or per quarter?

▶ Could you invest more if you could count on greater profits as a result?

▶ Have you examined media approaches for your business?

▶ List three ways you let people know about your business.

Worksheet: Selecting Proper Media for Purpose and Budget

Print Media

1. Which of the following are most appropriate for my product or service?

   ☐ Brochures
   ☐ Directory Yellow Pages
   ☐ Flyers (hand delivered)
   ☐ Flyers (bulk mail)
   ☐ Letters sent by direct mail
   ☐ Magazine ads
   ☐ Newspaper ads
   ☐ A combination of two or more print media (describe) _____
   _____

2. Which can I afford to use often enough for my initial marketing effort?

   _____

3. Which will reach all or most, but will not "overshoot" my target group or groups?

   _____

Audio (sound) Media

1. Which of the following are most appropriate for my product or service?

   ☐ Local Radio
   ☐ National Radio
   ☐ Telemarketing

2. Which can I afford to use often enough for my initial marketing effort?

   _____

3. Which will reach, but not "overshoot" my target group(s)?

   _____

TRACK YOUR RESULTS AND MODIFY YOUR MARKETING PLAN

The last step in developing a workable, cost effective marketing plan is to track the results of your tentative plan for a few weeks or months, assess its effectiveness, and modify it. This process, which usually takes several hours, allows you to eliminate whatever doesn't work and identify what does. From that point on, you can concentrate your time, efforts and money on the media, techniques and schedules that increase your client base, number of clients and profits.

You can simplify the process considerably by setting up file folders to hold the data necessary to evaluate your initial plan: the cost of each approach, frequency of use and effectiveness in generating new business over a pre-established period of time. One file folder for each approach and/or technique involved will make it relatively easy to assess the value of each.

The rest of this chapter details the procedure for accurately assessing costs and determining when to eliminate unprofitable marketing approaches. If you now have a marketing or advertising plan in operation, or have had one in the recent past, it will help to locate whatever records are available, and refer to them as you read.

Determine the Real Cost of New Business Gained from Marketing

Only after you determine the actual cost involved will you really know how much the new business is costing your company, and therefore how effective it is. A number of small business owners say that it costs only a few dollars in phone calls and postage, plus the time spent in a couple of appointments, to generate a new contract worth thousands of dollars. But those costs probably represented only the tip of the iceberg. It may have required only a few calls to that one company, but what about all the nonproductive calls made to potential customers within the same time period? Those are also part of the cost of gaining that lucrative contract.

The method of figuring these real costs is the same, regardless of the nature of your business. Try figuring your marketing costs on a quarterly or semi-annual basis, as follows:

▶ *Costs:* For a given period, add together the cost of all marketing phone calls, the money paid for telemarketing or ads, all postage for mailing samples, flyers, etc., all clerical time spent preparing mailings, time spent in generating new leads, all costs of envelopes and other materials, and the cost of your time spent traveling and on appointments with potential clients. To do this efficiently, keep certain records separately—postage for mailing packets, for example; over the years, it will simplify your costing procedure immensely.

▶ *New Business Generated from Marketing:* You may get some new business not connected to your marketing efforts. If so, do not count that new business. Other than that, total up the gross dollar amount of all new business generated from marketing during that same time period.

▶ *Marketing Cost:* You can use a simple hand calculator to figure what percentage of the new business gross figure went to the total cost of marketing. If, for example, you spend $125 to get $500 in new business, your marketing cost is 25 percent of the gross. Other small firms may have marketing costs of 15 to 40 percent plus per year. Whatever your costs, the question to ask yourself or your accountant is whether or not you can make a profit after deducting the costs. You will be able to determine this, no matter what your marketing cost percentage turns out to be.

Eliminate Unprofitable and/or Ineffective Media and Approaches

You may love the idea of having your company identified in newspaper ads. But if they're not bringing in new business or not *enough* business to cover the cost of the ads and earn a profit, drop them. To make decisions like this, you have to be able to track the pulling power of any given approach: discount coupons for retail products, cut-offs returned for additional information, questions to new customers about where they heard of your company, telemarketing records, phone inquiries and membership fees, plus time spent at organizational meetings. These records don't have to be perfect—in fact, they can't be—but they must be reasonably accurate and complete enough to allow you to assess the effectiveness of each part of your marketing plan.

When to Eliminate an Approach After you find the least effective approaches, you face the question of whether to eliminate them now or give them more time to become effective. There is no hard and fast rule for this. Sometimes I think gut feelings work about as well as any system for deciding how long a trial period should be—although any number of experts would be happy to dispute this with me. I am sure that over a period of time, experience with various approaches will tell you when you've invested enough time and money in a given approach or plan.

Do keep in mind that all marketing requires some investment in time and money before it works. In other words, avoid the too-little-too-late syndrome. It's better to allow a given plan to run a bit too long, than not long enough. Despite marked differences in approach and effectiveness, the examples that follow illustrate two important marketing principles related to when a program has run long enough:

1. When a particular part of your marketing plan has been in effect long enough to demonstrate its ineffectiveness, drop it! Don't send good money after bad.

2. What will work and what won't can be difficult, if not impossible to determine in advance. It's sometimes equally difficult to account for why only one of two equally logical approaches works for you.

Two manufacturers of similar types of machine parts, located in approximately the same industrial area and similar in size, number of items in their product lines and selling prices, had both been in business between five and ten years. Both pursued two marketing approaches: 2 × 4 inch boxed ads in trade magazines, and several sales people to generate, as well as follow up on, leads and inquiries. After about a year, one company dropped all ads except those in one magazine, finding them "virtually worthless"; the other expanded its trade journal advertising considerably and reduced its sales force to one person. An exhaustive analysis might reveal why their results differed so much, but the owners of both companies are still mystified, although their individual, modified plans became exceedingly cost effective.

A Variety of Techniques: Wholesale Firms Wholesale firms typically use the same media as manufacturers for marketing (trade journals and sales people); many also spend larger sums on trade show presentations and mailers to regular customers, especially to introduce a new line of products. These approaches are likely to be most cost effective for them.

Retail Sales Firms Retail sales firms are another matter entirely, since both their products and their geographical locations differ considerably. A mom-and-pop grocery store in a middle-class-to-affluent suburb spends most of its marketing budget on flyers to advertise weekly specials. These are circulated by a bulk mail company, along with other similar flyers, to the neighborhoods selected by the store owners. When this store first opened, the owners sent out broadside mailers once a month, delivered by a company that hired people to go from door to door. This didn't bring in much business, so they increased the frequency. When new business was still slow in coming, they switched to specialized bulk mail flyers and have found those effective ever since.

Neighborhood Businesses Another retail mom-and-pop store in a much less affluent neighborhood learned quickly that mailers, even with coupons, were not effective in bringing in new business. Because their customers live within walking or close driving distance of the store, they rely strictly on local advertising; window ads and occasional seasonal banners to attract attention, help keep regular customers and help build new business. Once in a great while, and only when part of the cost is paid by one of their distributors, they distribute store coupons for certain products locally, using a door-to-door delivery service.

To build business during their first two or three years in business, a delicatessen sent out a variety of bulk mail and hand delivered flyers. Now that they have a reputation for quality and value over a fairly widespread area, they no longer use either mailers or flyers. They run a weekly ad, modest in size, in the food supplement of a local newspaper. This store needs no other marketing or advertising to keep its name before the public.

Consulting Firms: Networking   Two management consulting firms, one in financial services and the other in human resources training, have absolute faith in networking through professional and community organizations. Networking has always been effective for them so they've had no reason to change or to add to their present marketing approaches. A third firm, which offers human resource management training, has a marketing plan based almost entirely on telemarketing, although the partners do a limited amount of networking. This company began by emphasizing networking; as that approach became increasingly time-consuming, they tried telemarketing, which proved to be consistently more effective. They have now expanded telemarketing into a full-scale operation that has nearly doubled the firm's geographical area, as well as its business.

The examples in this chapter, however limited, demonstrate the need to track your marketing efforts and modify your approaches until you develop a plan that brings you the amount and kind of new business you want. And a sound marketing plan will do just that.

Your Turn

Answer the following:

► Do you know if you have gained any new business from marketing?

► Do you have any way to determine how your customers find your business?

► List any feedback mechanism you have in place to learn how customers have found your business.

Worksheet: Tracking Marketing Costs and Returns

Time Period: (Month, Quarter, Six-Months, etc.)

Dollar Amount	Cost	Return	Cost	Return	Cost	Return	Cost	Return
451–500								
401–450								
351–400								
301–350								
251–300								
201–250								
151–200								
101–150								
76–100								
51– 75								
25– 50								
Below 25								

Media & Approach (Samples)	Yellow Pages Ad Directory:	Trade Journal Ad # of Issues:	Bulk Mail Flyer # of Pieces	Telemarketing # of Hours:
	_____	_____	_____	_____

ASK YOURSELF

► As step one in identifying your marketing target groups, discuss your best sources for gathering information about your present customers/clients.

► In your business, describe an appropriate marketing trial flight. Comment on the time you need to allow before you can expect to track the results.

CHAPTER
FIVE

EXPANDING
YOUR
BUSINESS

DECIDE HOW MUCH AND HOW FAST?

Guiding Principle: A healthy business is sure to grow. Make sure you control how much and how fast it expands.

It's probably hard to believe that after you have met and solved the numerous problems connected to operating your business and it is up and running smoothly, you need to make yet another set of major decisions. This time, those decisions concern the degree and rate at which you want it to expand. It's true, though. One of the unavoidable facts of business life is that you spend much of your decision-making time performing a balancing act, sometimes between a rock and a hard place, and often between two or more equally desirable options.

An indispensable prerequisite to expansion is to give careful thought to how large you want your company to become. While some owners of small businesses view their present sizes as stepping stones to really large firms, many do not. These are the people who want to run their own businesses. They have strong desires to control the destiny of those businesses for the foreseeable future. As a guide to determine the optimum size for your company, ask yourself the following questions:

▶ Do you want it to be larger than it is now, but still small enough for you to run it yourself?

▶ Do you want it to be big enough to require a partner or other additional full-time management person?

▶ Do you want it to be double the size it is now?

▶ Are you hoping to expand into a large corporation?

Your answers to these questions will clarify your goals for your company's future. They will help you determine, at least in part, the rate at which you expand.

Once you have reached a decision on the future size of your company, you are ready to concentrate on the best rate of expansion: expand too fast and you can fall head over heels; too slow and you could stumble trying to keep up. The business pages of newspapers are full of stories about small businesses that went belly-up because they got too large, too fast and were so far in debt they couldn't climb out. Those same papers are equally full of stories about companies that went under because they didn't expand fast enough to keep up with the demand for their products or services. As the owner of a small business, you aren't likely to hit the headlines, but if you make one of the same mistakes, you could come to the same end. This chapter will help you expand your company to the size you want, at the rate you decide is best. You will

► Increase Your Working Capital and Cash Reserves

► Expand Your Product Line or Services

► Increase Your Human Resource Network

► Add Equipment and Space When Necessary

INCREASE YOUR WORKING CAPITAL AND PROFIT MARGIN

Those first months—perhaps years—of working under constant pressure to make ends meet and maintain a cash flow at something above a trickle may be challenging and exciting. But if that unremitting pressure continues for too long, it will interfere with your ability to develop the degree of confidence and financial stability that are essential for expanding your business properly.

One of the problems of new businesses of any size—a problem that will come as no surprise to most small business owners— is inadequate capital. In fact, according to the gurus who specialize in helping struggling companies to make a turn- around, undercapitalization is the single greatest reason that so many businesses fail in their first year or two. Fortunately, there is more than one way to build a cash reserve large enough to assure a steady cash flow and allow room for implementing plans to expand. There are risk venture capi- talists, of course, but they are not exactly underfoot; even if they were, the cost of such money can be exorbitant. More practical approaches are to build a cash margin over time, to establish a line of credit at your bank and, if possible, to increase your profit margin.

Build a Cash Margin of Three to Six Months' Operating Expenses

Operating expenses are what it costs to meet your break-even point. If it regularly costs you $2,000 a month for fixed and other standard expenses, you will need a minimum margin of $6,000 and a maximum margin of $12,000. When you are able to keep this far ahead, fairly consistently, your stress level and blood pressure will drop considerably, while your efficiency and production rate will increase significantly; it's hard to concentrate if there's a nagging worry in the back of your mind about paying next month's rent and phone bill.

Methods of reaching this happy plateau of security vary with the type of business; the majority of small businesses build their reserve fund over a period of time. Key words are *planning* and *consistency.* Waiting for a windfall from a fairy godmother to fall in your lap does not rank high on the scale of successful plans. What *does* work is a careful assessment of weekly, monthly or quarterly profits, coupled with patient, steady efforts to set aside a certain sum or percentage regularly, until your reserve is in place. It may be easier, or less painful than you think.

A manufacturing firm put 1 percent of its quarterly net profits into a separate bank account; if there were no profits in the particular quarter, no money went into that account. Within a year and a half, the firm had its reserve margin. The owner of a shoe store did it much the same way, except that a specific sum of money went into the special account each week. The owner was able to do it this way because weekly income was relatively stable. A father and son who owned a printing company received payment for two large orders at about the same time; they set aside one of the payments as a first install-ment on their reserve. After that, whenever a similar situation existed, they added to the reserve with all or part of one payment—an unorthodox method, but one that worked because the owners were consistent in how they allocated money to the special fund. However you accomplish it, once you have your reserve in place, you will have a foundation of security for expanding your company.

Establish a Line of Credit Before You Need It

Nothing will destroy your banker's faith in you and your ability to run a business faster than arriving at the bank wild-eyed and in urgent need of cash. This is a situation where planning ahead is crucial if you will need extra money when you are ready to expand, or even if a flat economy or other temporary setback means that you require extra funds.

If you haven't been in business long enough to have established a track record for dependability and profitability, the bank will undoubtedly ask for collateral to guarantee a line of credit: a mortgage on your house, your right arm up to the elbow, or your firstborn child. If there is no other way to get a line of credit, base it on collateral. But ask that the requirement for collateral be eliminated after a year, provided you prove to be a reliable and responsible borrower.

A better way, if you can manage it, is to demonstrate a steady rate of profit or increase in gross profit over a period of two or three years; then, ask for a moderate amount of credit even if the bank is willing to allow you more. Or, if your business is one where accounts receivable are payable in 30 to 60 days, base your line of credit on accounts receivable. This has several advantages. For one, you can borrow against virtually certain future income that is a form of collateral. For another, it helps you to maintain a steady cash flow while you are working on large contracts or projects. Finally, borrowing against future income reduces the temptation to borrow too much.

No matter how you succeed in establishing a line of credit, its greatest advantage, perhaps, is that you will have a source available for funds when you are ready to expand your business.

CAUTION: During expansion, resist any and all urges to plunge headlong into a vast scheme requiring you to borrow to the limit. That way lies disaster.

Increase Your Profit Margin

You may think you have already established the optimal balance between costs and prices or fee structure for your company. But costs have a habit of inching upwards almost imperceptibly; it's wise to examine the gap periodically, with an eye towards increasing your profit margin. Also, small business owners sometimes hesitate to increase prices, for fear they can't match the competition and will lose business as a result. In our economy, however, inflation is always present to some degree; if you don't keep your profits high enough to compensate for inflation, you will find yourself falling behind, unable to afford expansion, even when you see a need for it. Provided that your price increases are reasonable, moderate and in keeping with what the market will bear for your product line or services, make it a point to keep your profits up and, when possible, increase the margin of profit.

This is easier to achieve in some fields than in others. In manufacturing, increased costs for materials, labor and services are highly visible. When your own prices go up because of these increases, an extra dollar here and there will not outrage your customers who are accustomed to an expanding market. That extra amount to increase your profit margin can also help you expand when you are ready.

While increases in costs in wholesale and retail sales are not usually visible, to customers especially, everyone is aware that inflation exists. As long as you don't increase all your prices overnight, your customers will continue to buy from you. Also, in sales you can frequently use a technique that large companies use all the time. Before a price increase, put the item or items on sale at the price that allows buyers to really save money. Then, after the sale, add the increase to the "regular" price. This is such a common device for making price increases that I have developed a habit of buying large quantities of supplies I use often when they do go on sale— because I am reasonably sure the regular price will go up soon.

In service fields, the usual way to keep up with costs and increase your profit margin is to increase your hourly rate, the price per service, or whatever applies to your business. Some consulting firms increase their hourly rate for new clients only or for clients whose volume of business is small. Other service companies—those in the enviable position of having a large volume of business—wait until they have more business than they can handle and then raise their rates for all clients; those who can't, or won't, pay the new rate simply go elsewhere.

Regardless of your type of business, it is important to think in terms of increasing your profit margin, not merely compensating for increased costs; in this way, you will build a reserve that will be available when your marketing plan has brought in enough new business to allow you to expand.

Your Turn   *Answer the following:*

► Rank the following in the order of their feasibility for your company:

- Building cash margin

- Establishing a line of credit

- Increasing your profit margin

► Do you have a cash margin of three to six months' operating expenses?

► Have you established a line of credit?

EXPAND YOUR PRODUCT LINE OR SERVICES

Adding new products or services in keeping with your plans for the future of your company is an excellent way to expand. Chapter 1 contains information on adding new products or services as a means of quality improvement; you may wish to review that chapter. Now, however, you will be examining your present offerings with expansion in mind. This new objective requires not only a different perspective, but also specific knowledge of what your competition offers. It requires the ability to identify new ways to fill another market niche or appeal to a new client base and geographical area.

Achieving your current objective calls for a study of your present market base to find out what your customers or clients might buy from you. Such a study can be very informal; after you have identified a number of possibilities for new offerings, send or give a list of them to your customers with a request to check the ones they would "probably" buy, "might" buy, or "would not" buy. Keep your list simple; to ensure a good response, couple it with some kind of offer—a discount or other enticement that makes it worthwhile for customers to respond. If you intend to expand on a large scale, carefully design your marketing plan before launching new products or services. Regardless of what you ultimately decide to add to your present line, it is important to move cautiously at first. Stick with one or two new offerings until you see how customers respond; add others according to demand and your ability to finance and produce them.

Identify or Create Another Market Niche

This requires creative thinking. If you manufacture, sell or service widgets similar to the widgets produced, sold and/or services by your competition, it isn't easy to recognize another niche in the widget market. Brainstorming, alone or with a trusted partner, helps. Begin by asking yourself if there are any possible variations on widgets that you have overlooked:

- ► Sizes

- ► Colors

- ► Added bells and whistles

- ► New functions or uses

- ► A stripped down version

- ► Other materials

As you list variations, include even the wildest, most impractical ones; great ideas sometimes arrive in strange ways. The trick is to encourage your mind to roam freely around widget country for a while, unfettered by requirements of any kind. You can always eliminate unproductive or unsuitable ideas later. In the meantime, create as comprehensive a list of possibilities as possible. Afterwards, go through the list and select the most promising ideas first. Give these—perhaps only two or three—serious thought before going through your original list again, this time selecting the next best ideas, regardless of whether or not you think they are practical or necessary, etc. Continue this process until you have created a refined list with the best ideas at the top and the really impossible or idiotic ones eliminated altogether.

The next step is to go through your refined list, this time with an eye to determining which ideas are practical enough for solid consideration—not too expensive, for example, or too time consuming for your company. Out of this process you will almost surely generate at least one workable idea for a new product or service.

The partners who own and operate a company that manufactures standard and deluxe metal widgets in several sizes had been trying to expand their line without success. In desperation, they decided to try the brainstorming process, but as they sat down together to start a list, one partner said there was no need to consider different colors; all widgets were made of metal the same grey color. At that, the other partner said, "That's it! Colors. A different color for each size." And, although they went ahead with their list, at the end they decided to produce widgets in a range of anodized finishes, a different color for each size to make identification easier. Their customers love the innovation because it has reduced errors and increased the production rate; the manufacturing company loves it because business has increased almost 30 percent.

A small electronics store located in a suburban mini-mall had done very well for three years, selling a variety of electronic household widgets. Because their product lines are exceptionally comprehensive, the owners didn't see how they could reasonably expand by appealing to another market. However, when a customer who had returned a widget with a defective cord remarked that cords were a problem with widgets in general, the owners realized they had a possible new market: specialized widget cords in every available size and type. Normally, people have to look in hardware and home improvement stores for these items, often searching in several places before finding what they need. Now, the electronics widget store has established a "cord corner." They serve regular customers and have brought in new ones who came originally to buy a widget cord replacement.

One firm that services a number of office widgets has created a new market niche and expanded by adding a product line at the same time. One service they are often called on to perform involves client use of the wrong type of lubrication or inferior operating supplies for their widget. After servicing a particular widget machine, service technicians routinely told clients what to use in the future. Recently, however, they began stocking their two service vans with the best and most wanted supplies for widgets they serviced. In a matter of months, they found themselves with a profitable market and a line of products as well as services.

Identify Different Functions and Uses for Your Products and Services

This method, while it is not applicable to every type of business, can help you expand in two ways: by increasing the ways your present buyers use what you offer, and by increasing the range of buyers who might need or want your products or services. What you must look for, of course, is a logical extension of present functions. You would hardly suggest that your customers use cooking widgets for digging holes in the garden. Nor would you want children to use your toy widgets as hammers for driving nails into the wall. The trick is to look at your offerings through new eyes, or pay close attention to what clients tell you they use your No. 1 widget for, other than the purpose you intended.

A classic example of this type of expansion is the 3M Post-it™ tapes, currently inundating the market in every conceivable size, shape and color. They were "invented" by accident when the 3M research people were trying to develop a better glue. When the ones they came up with wouldn't stick tight enough, they discarded the samples. A clerk in the office promptly began using them as temporary tags and flags on papers. The rest, as they say, is history. Every office in the country is papered with Post-its™; at this moment, I can look around my office and see them used as index tabs, bin labels, memos and phone messages, to name a few. You may not devise a new function as dramatic as the Post-it™ phenomenon, but try it anyway. You might be surprised.

One manufacturer of sets of plastic drawers in a frame for storing screws, nails and other small machine parts was told by a customer that, at home, his wife used several sets of the drawers in different sizes to store herbs and condiments, such as small dried peppers, ginger and garlic. Asked why she used these instead of conventional containers, she said she could see through the clear plastic, they held more of the ones she used most, and took up very little counter space. Ultimately, this happy little piece of information led the manufacturer to expand into a highly profitable and entirely new market.

There are many examples of toys used as elements in sculpture or other three dimensional art—utilitarian objects like buttons used as decorations, and even various shapes of pasta gilded and used as Christmas tree ornaments. Many of these objects, originally sold for one purpose, take on new life in another way altogether. Take a close look at whatever you sell to see if it could have other, marketable uses; if so, determine whether you could capitalize on that new use to expand in another direction.

In service fields, new functions and uses are not as common or easy to identify, but they do exist. A consulting firm, called in about running a seminar on the client's new phone system, thought the purpose was to train employees how to use it. But it turned out that, while most employees knew how to use the equipment, they really needed to be motivated sufficiently to use its advanced functions, including voice mail messages. The consultants, somewhat bemused by this twist in their usual work, designed what looked like a technical training seminar; it was, in fact, a motivational one.

In my own business, the manuals we write normally have one of two functions: to train employees in how to operate equipment, or to help buyers assemble or use a product they buy. However, one client, for whom we have written a number of basic equipment operating manuals for training new employees, asked us to produce a special topic index for one of these manuals—something that is seldom necessary. When I asked about it, the client told me that this manual, with its slightly larger than normal print and open, wide spaced format, was ideal as a textbook for their employees who had limited command of English! Desperate for skilled labor, they were recruiting people new to this country. As part of their orientation, they put them through a short, intense course in the English language while they taught them about their jobs.

Your Turn   ***Answer the following:***

► List two or three new products or services you might want to add to your present offerings.

► List two other functions or uses for your products or services.

EXPAND YOUR HUMAN RESOURCES NETWORK

Clearly, as your business expands, you will need more people to do part of the work and to provide certain services. Go slowly. Labor costs represent a significant investment, usually the most expensive part of any business operation. You want to choose wisely among available options. It's not a problem to spend money on services you seldom use—printing of letterheads and business cards, for example. The problem is how, when and how much to use other people to perform regular or frequently needed tasks such as mailing bills, doing word processing and other clerical work that supports your business.

There are two ways to go: use outside services and independent contractors to perform certain types of work, or hire full or part-time employees. Your decision will depend on several factors: the rate at which you are expanding, the amount of money you can afford to spend, and the amount and kind of help you want. If you are working a full forty hour week, you may or may not need much help. If you are on overload, working more than a forty hour week and having trouble getting everything done, you have to expand your human resource network in a way that is both efficient and affordable. This chapter explores the options open to small business owners and some cost effective ways to implement them.

Use Outside Services

This option, often one of the best for a business that wants to expand on a limited budget, allows you to delegate specific parts of your business operation to firms and individuals who specialize in the work you need. Hiring accountants or CPAs to do the business records and taxes is invaluable when you have neither the expertise nor the time to devote to them. Payroll services who actually hire your employees and lease them back to you can also remove a time-consuming, difficult task from your shoulders. Mailing and billing tasks, reports and other typing or word processing can frequently be done better, faster and cheaper by an outside service than by a temporary or part-time person in your office.

Since most manufacturers use employees to produce their products, these firms have a multitude of time cards, payroll records and other bookkeeping to perform. For them, an outside service, hired on a contract basis and functioning like another department in the company, can be a highly efficient, cost effective option.

In retail sales, distributors, acting as intermediaries between manufacturers and the sales outlet, allow the owner to purchase many products and kinds of products on one order. If the volume of sales is large enough, retailers can also make excellent use of bookkeeping services to handle supplier invoices, inventory records and the like, on a regular basis.

Service firms, themselves specialists, often use a variety of highly specialized services related to their business. An industrial psychologist "rents" sophisticated computer time to perform statistical analysis, for example. My own company uses word processing, telemarketing and clerical services that we require often, but not for enough hours to warrant hiring extra employees. A management consulting firm that, for its first ten years spent an average of two hours a week on book-keeping records, now uses outside accounting and bookkeeping services. In retrospect, the owners believe the time they spent doing this type of work was a false economy; they now realize they could have spent their time more profitably in networking or developing their seminars.

Use Independent Contractors

Independent contractors, like outside services, can extend your human resource network when you need help with special projects. Make sure that independent contractors meet two criteria, in particular: they regularly do the type of work that they are performing for you, and they do not work under your direct supervision or control. If you need special help from time to time, then outside contractors may be a cost-effective alternative to hiring an employee.

Manufacturing companies find it cost-effective to use sub-contractors to manufacture components that go into their products. Also, they may use outside contractors on a limited basis as sales representatives, although an independent sales-person cannot be relied on to meet a specific schedule for sales calls or to devote a certain number of hours regularly to sell your products.

The most common use for outside contractors in sales is as sales representatives on the same limited basis that manu-facturing companies use them. Otherwise, sales firms are more likely to use outside service firms and employees.

It is in this type of business that independent contractors must often work. Bookkeeping and accounting firms regularly use certain contractors for special projects; word processing ser-vices subcontract some of their work when they are rushed. Other service businesses regularly use outside contractors to supplement their staff, considering it an extremely effective means of extending their human resource network and expanding their business at a reasonable cost.

Hire Part-time or Full-time Employees

While this is an expensive, major step for many small businesses, it can be an effective way to extend your human resource network and expand your business, especially if you plan to significantly increase the size of your company. Hiring part-time employees works well if you are able to find a person who wants to work the number of hours you need. Otherwise, it may be just as efficient to use someone from a temporary employment agency, provided the job does not call for special skills or training not available from an agency.

Hiring one or more full-time employees is another matter. Following certain guidelines can help you decide when it's time to hire someone:

► Assuming you have no employees yet and you are already working a forty hour week, do you need at least an additional twenty hours of work? If so, you may be ready to hire an employee. Part of the reasoning here is that what you could accomplish in twenty hours will probably take an employee twice as long to complete.

► Is the work of such nature that an outside service or contractor is not suited or available to do it? If so, an employee is the answer.

► Can you afford to pay the benefits, taxes, workmen's compensation and other expenses, in addition to an employee's base pay? If so, then you can afford to hire someone.

► Do your plans for expansion make it possible for an employee to later advance to a higher paying position? While this guideline isn't as essential as the preceding ones, it's worth considering what sort of future a full-time employee can expect with your firm. If you spend the necessary time to locate the type and amount of extra help your company needs for expansion, you will discover practical ways to expand your human resource network to meet your company's needs, without excessive costs.

Answer the following:

► How long is your typical work week?

- Under 40 hours
- About 40 hours
- Over 40 hours

► How often do you fall behind on essential tasks?

- Seldom
- Often
- Always

► Which kinds of tasks usually fall behind?

- Production
- Purchasing
- Record keeping
- Advance scheduling
- Other (specify)

ADD EQUIPMENT AND SPACE WHEN NECESSARY

A conservative but sensible approach to adding equipment and increasing space is best. If you are a "shopaholic" who buys everything new on the market just because it's there, or if your head is filled with rose-colored visions of megasized corporate offices, you probably shouldn't make decisions about what to buy and when to move to larger quarters. I know of at least two manufacturing companies and several sales and service firms that put themselves out of business for just these reasons, while the owners were still feeling the euphoria of early success.

On the other hand, don't allow yourself to continue to work with outdated, unreliable equipment, in quarters so cramped for space you can't find a place to store an extra paperclip. A floor covering firm that had an enormous number of carpeting, vinyl and tile samples had so little space that it took the owners twice as long as it should to locate samples they wanted to show customers. They were trying to stay within a limited budget, of course; when they finally realized how inefficient their operation had become, and moved into larger quarters, they discovered that their attractive new showroom was also bringing in attractive new business.

Expansion always involves a balancing act between expense and need, especially when it comes to paying for, often costly, equipment and space. More equipment and space can require sizable sums of money. Don't despair. When you've made the decision to invest in additional equipment and/or space, after carefully working through the cost-versus-need equation, you will be able to expand to meet your future, as well as present, requirements.

Add Equipment

It's important to buy new equipment in time to meet your needs. If you buy it too far ahead of time, you're wasting money; you may not have the right kind of equipment when the time comes that you do need it. If you wait too long to buy it, you're also probably wasting money in repair bills, excessive operating costs and reduced production efficiency. A checklist can help you determine when it's necessary to replace an old copier or piece of manufacturing equipment, or to add another one:

☐ Is the equipment often out of order?

☐ Are maintenance costs increasing considerably?

☐ Does the equipment operate so slowly that you have work backed up?

☐ Are you having difficulty meeting delivery schedules?

☐ Do new versions of the equipment have additional functions that you need now?

☐ Will a new piece of equipment meet your future as well as your present needs?

If you answered *yes* to half or more of these questions, it's time to replace or add a new piece of equipment.

Consider fax machines, which are widely used in many businesses. A manufacturing company that sold its products to local distributors had a simple, relatively inexpensive fax machine for sending and receiving inquiries, copies of invoices, lists of materials, etc. When the company expanded its territory to include several distributors in the neighboring state, fax transmission costs began to climb. The machine was slow, the copies were hard to read and repair costs increased. Finally, an exasperated clerk who wanted to send a number of documents on a day when the fax was not working, handed the owner five brochures detailing specific features of new fax machines: delayed transmission, ability to send thirty documents at a time, a memory for receiving transmissions when the paper ran out at midnight—as it always seemed to—much faster transmission and readable copies. While the new machines were far more expensive than the company's present fax, the clerk pointed out that faster transmissions and delayed transmissions at night meant lower fax bills; the other features would increase the efficiency of all their communications operations. The owner got the message; the office got a new fax machine; the clerk got a raise. Three years later, the new fax machine is still serving the company's needs.

A neighborhood fast-food takeout establishment did not have a fax and saw no need for one. Then a new manager arrived. One of her first actions was to buy a fax machine, capable of handling a number of transmissions rapidly. Her second action was to splash big banners across the front of the store, telling people to fax their lunch orders for pickup without waiting. Her third action was to paper the local offices and industrial complexes with flyers containing the same message as the banners, including the fax number. Business literally doubled while the crush of people waiting at the counter at noon was cut in half.

My own company got along just fine without a fax machine for seven years. Then, when I was thinking of getting one, I realized that to be efficient I'd need a top-end model with quite a few bells and whistles. About that time, a client with plants in several states ordered another manual. That did it. In my business, we have to send review drafts back and forth, sometimes several times. I already knew that the phone bills would be high; the fax salesperson assured me that faxed transmissions, especially those sent at night by delayed transmission, cost less than most phone calls. This turned out to be the understatement of the year. I've never spent so little, to accomplish so much, in so little time. And my expensive machine, except for the one major problem described earlier, has been a reliable right arm ever since.

Increase Space

Sometimes you can increase the efficiency of the space you already occupy if you change the arrangement of the work stations, furniture, machines, etc. If you think this might work for you, an efficiency consultant or office space designer could save you the cost of moving to larger quarters. Otherwise, it's as important to make your move to larger quarters at the right time as it is to buy equipment when you need it. Again, a checklist can help you make a sound decision:

☐ If you want to add a new employee, furniture or equipment, would you have a hard time finding the necessary space?

☐ Is your storage room or area crammed with supplies spilling out onto the floor?

☐ Is every desk and available work surface stacked with folders, equipment and other items?

☐ Do you have to search through a dozen locations before you find what you are looking for?

☐ Is the general appearance of your office and/or plant neat or cluttered?

☐ If you had more space would it be useful to you in the future as well as now?

Again, if you answered *yes* to half or more of these questions, it's undoubtedly time to increase your space. If your place really looks like the descriptions above, it's past time to move.

When you decide to move to larger quarters, regardless of whether you're looking for offices, office-plus-plant facilities or plant facilities only, you must make two other decisions *before* you start looking at actual sites. First, establish a minimum and maximum amount of rent you can afford to pay. This may require a session or two with your accountant and/or banker, but it's essential to establish the limits ahead of time to avoid spending money you don't have. The other preliminary decision has to do with how much space you need now and for at least several years into the future—too little and you'll incur moving costs again, sooner than you should; too much, and you'll be wasting money you could use elsewhere. Granted, both of these decisions involve some guesswork but, by assessing how much more space you actually need now and estimating your future rate of growth, according to your rate and amount of expansion since you started the business, you will arrive at some practical figures.

When you start looking at what's on the market, you may have to make some trade-offs; the ideal rent may be for less space than you want, for instance. Provided the difference between your preliminary estimates and the realities you discover aren't too great, you may decide to either spend a little more or accept somewhat less space than you want. A checklist will assist you in finding the right place for your expanding company:

☐ Is the location right? The best possible space in an inconvenient or otherwise unsuitable area is not the right one. It is not by accident that real estate people say that the three most important considerations are *location, location* and *location*. Make sure that the new quarters are convenient for your customers, your supplier and yourself.

☐ Do the building and its surroundings project the image you wish to present? To a manufacturer of parts for the aerospace industry or a company whose customers seldom or never come to the office, image and appearance may carry little or no weight. To a company that makes cosmetics or a management consulting service, image will be crucial.

☐ Do the building and its grounds appear to be well maintained? Even if image is not important, clean, neat premises that do not need obvious repair are extremely important. You don't want a landlord who fails to make necessary repairs!

☐ Is the size within or nearly within the limits you have established? If not, look elsewhere. A thriving hobby shop moved into "ideal" new quarters—great location, great image, great everything except it was 100 square feet smaller than the owner wanted. In one year, the store had to move again to accommodate a new product line that had hit the public's fancy.

☐ Is the interior space arrangement suitable? Quarters with the proper amount of space may still not be right if the rooms, offices, etc., are not arranged according to your needs, or the prospective landlord is not willing to make the necessary changes for a reasonable price.

☐ Are there other disadvantages? Undesirable neighbors, limited parking space, not enough restrooms or lack of nearby places to have lunch can lessen the desirability of an otherwise satisfactory location. A retail store located in a nice local business area with a good size parking lot discovered, after moving in, that behind their parking lot was an apartment house where noisy gangs of teenagers habitually congregated—and decorated nearby buildings with graffiti.

☐ Can you negotiate the kind and length of lease that you want? If you need a shorter or longer lease than the landlord is willing to sign, or there are other conditions you really don't want to live with, it's best to look elsewhere. A lease is binding; conditions not to your liking now may grow into major irritants in a few months or years.

After you have weighed and balanced the advantages and disadvantages according to this checklist, you probably haven't located the perfect new offices and/or plant facilities, but you will certainly have new quarters that are appropriate for your company, now as well as into the future.

Your Turn

Answer the following:

► If you had enough money, which would you add right away?

  • New equipment

  • Space

  • Both

► Is your workspace cluttered?

► Do you have any kind of organizational system at work?

ASK YOURSELF

► Discuss the most basic decision you must make before you consider the specifics of expanding your business.

► Which of the following represent my best source(s) for increasing working capital? Why?

- Line of credit at my bank

- Accumulated Cash Margin

- Increased profit margin

► Identify and describe one specific item or service you could add to your present offerings.

► If and when you need more help, will it be best for your company to add one or more employees or to use outside independent contractors? Why?

► Considering your time, energy, financial and human resources, discuss the best rate of expansion for your company.

AFTERWORD

Now that you have read this book, you have taken a journey that covers considerable territory applicable to small businesses everywhere. You can take comfort in knowing that others have met challenges like the ones you may be facing right now. You need no longer feel that you are wandering alone in an uncharted landscape, inhabited solely by the directors of mega corporations.

The guidelines, real life examples and the practice exercises in this book have given you an opportunity to garner ideas and practical strategies to apply or adapt to your own business, now or in the future. And you may already feel the exhilaration and sense of achievement that come to those with the courage and determination to strike out on their own.

However, this is not the end of your journey. You are ready to turn your Owner's Guide into a desk reference tool, a resource in the coming months and years, for additional help in directing your present business along the lines you want it to grow. If you find yourself bogged down by the many details of daily business operations, review Chapter 2; you may find a way to use your time more efficiently. Or if you are looking for a new approach to marketing or advertising, review Chapter 4 for ideas. Operating and perhaps expanding your business into a larger, even more successful enterprise is a splendid journey.

Happy traveling!

ABOUT THE AUTHOR

Over the last thirty years, Betty M. Bivins has had the checkered career typical of writers: newspaper reporter, blue book editor of a trade journal in Chicago, manager of a finance company, teacher of literature and composition, English adviser to secondary schools in the Los Angeles Unified School District (LAUSD) and, for the last ten years, President of the WRITE Group, Inc., a technical writing company in Frazier Park, California.

Her writing background, in addition to a number of magazine articles in such varied publications as *Cat Fancy* and the English Journal, includes: two secondary composition instructional guides and a reading guide for the LAUSD; one of four authors of a secondary history textbook, *Life and Liberty*, published by Scott, Foresman and Co.; two franchise manuals; and, as she puts it, "more technical manuals than I care to remember!"

ABOUT CRISP PUBLICATIONS

We hope that you enjoyed this book. If so, we have good news for you. This title is only one in the library of Crisp's best-selling books. Each of our books is easy to use and is obtainable at a very reasonable price.

Books are available from your distributor. A free catalog is available upon request from Crisp Publications, Inc., 1200 Hamilton Court, Menlo Park, California 94025. Phone: (415) 323-6100; Fax: (415) 323-5800.

Books are organized by general subject area.

Computer Series

Management Training